Think Stats

Allen B. Downey

O'REILLY®

Beijing · Cambridge · Farnham · Köln · Sebastopol · Tokyo

Think Stats

by Allen B. Downey

Published by O'Reilly Media, Inc., 1005 Gravenstein Highway North, Sebastopol, CA 95472.

O'Reilly books may be purchased for educational, business, or sales promotional use. Online editions are also available for most titles (*http://my.safaribooksonline.com*). For more information, contact our corporate/institutional sales department: (800) 998-9938 or *corporate@oreilly.com*.

Editor: Mike Loukides	**Cover Designer:** Karen Montgomery
Production Editor: Jasmine Perez	**Interior Designer:** David Futato
Proofreader: Jasmine Perez	**Illustrator:** Robert Romano

June 2011:   First Edition.

Revision History for the First Edition:

2011-06-30	First release
2011-09-21	Second release
2012-03-02	Third release
2012-05-15	Fourth release

See *http://oreilly.com/catalog/errata.csp?isbn=9781449307110* for release details.

ISBN: 978-1-449-30711-0

[LSI]

1337026873

Table of Contents

Preface

Why I Wrote This Book

Think Stats is a textbook for a new kind of introductory prob-stat class. It emphasizes the use of statistics to explore large datasets. It takes a computational approach, which has several advantages:

- Students write programs as a way of developing and testing their understanding. For example, they write functions to compute a least squares fit, residuals, and the coefficient of determination. Writing and testing this code requires them to understand the concepts and implicitly corrects misunderstandings.

- Students run experiments to test statistical behavior. For example, they explore the Central Limit Theorem (CLT) by generating samples from several distributions. When they see that the sum of values from a Pareto distribution doesn't converge to normal, they remember the assumptions the CLT is based on.

- Some ideas that are hard to grasp mathematically are easy to understand by simulation. For example, we approximate p-values by running Monte Carlo simulations, which reinforces the meaning of the p-value.

- Using discrete distributions and computation makes it possible to present topics like Bayesian estimation that are not usually covered in an introductory class. For example, one exercise asks students to compute the posterior distribution for the "German tank problem," which is difficult analytically but surprisingly easy computationally.

- Because students work in a general-purpose programming language (Python), they are able to import data from almost any source. They are not limited to data that has been cleaned and formatted for a particular statistics tool.

The book lends itself to a project-based approach. In my class, students work on a semester-long project that requires them to pose a statistical question, find a dataset that can address it, and apply each of the techniques they learn to their own data.

To demonstrate the kind of analysis I want students to do, the book presents a case study that runs through all of the chapters. It uses data from two sources:

- The National Survey of Family Growth (NSFG), conducted by the U.S. Centers for Disease Control and Prevention (CDC) to gather "information on family life, marriage and divorce, pregnancy, infertility, use of contraception, and men's and women's health." (See *http://cdc.gov/nchs/nsfg.htm*.)
- The Behavioral Risk Factor Surveillance System (BRFSS), conducted by the National Center for Chronic Disease Prevention and Health Promotion to "track health conditions and risk behaviors in the United States." (See *http://cdc.gov/BRFSS/*.)

Other examples use data from the IRS, the U.S. Census, and the Boston Marathon.

How I Wrote This Book

When people write a new textbook, they usually start by reading a stack of old textbooks. As a result, most books contain the same material in pretty much the same order. Often there are phrases, and errors, that propagate from one book to the next; Stephen Jay Gould pointed out an example in his essay, "The Case of the Creeping Fox Terrier."[1] I did not do that. In fact, I used almost no printed material while I was writing this book, for several reasons:

- My goal was to explore a new approach to this material, so I didn't want much exposure to existing approaches.
- Since I am making this book available under a free license, I wanted to make sure that no part of it was encumbered by copyright restrictions.
- Many readers of my books don't have access to libraries of printed material, so I tried to make references to resources that are freely available on the Internet.
- Proponents of old media think that the exclusive use of electronic resources is lazy and unreliable. They might be right about the first part, but I think they are wrong about the second, so I wanted to test my theory.

The resource I used more than any other is Wikipedia, the bugbear of librarians everywhere. In general, the articles I read on statistical topics were very good (although I made a few small changes along the way). I include references to Wikipedia pages throughout the book and I encourage you to follow those links; in many cases, the Wikipedia page picks up where my description leaves off. The vocabulary and notation in this book are generally consistent with Wikipedia, unless I had a good reason to deviate.

---

1. A breed of dog that is about half the size of a Hyracotherium (see *http://wikipedia.org/wiki/Hyracotherium*).

Other resources I found useful were Wolfram MathWorld and (of course) Google. I also used two books, David MacKay's *Information Theory, Inference, and Learning Algorithms*, which is the book that got me hooked on Bayesian statistics, and Press et al.'s *Numerical Recipes in C*. But both books are available online, so I don't feel too bad.

Contributor List

Please send email to *downey@allendowney.com* if you have a suggestion or correction. If I make a change based on your feedback, I will add you to the contributor list (unless you ask to be omitted).

If you include at least part of the sentence the error appears in, that makes it easy for me to search. Page and section numbers are fine, too, but not quite as easy to work with. Thanks!

- Lisa Downey and June Downey read an early draft and made many corrections and suggestions.
- Steven Zhang found several errors.
- Andy Pethan and Molly Farison helped debug some of the solutions, and Molly spotted several typos.
- Andrew Heine found an error in my error function.
- Dr. Nikolas Akerblom knows how big a Hyracotherium is.
- Alex Morrow clarified one of the code examples.
- Jonathan Street caught an error in the nick of time.
- Gábor Lipták found a typo in the book and the relay race solution.
- Many thanks to Kevin Smith and Tim Arnold for their work on plasTeX, which I used to convert this book to DocBook.
- George Caplan sent several suggestions for improving clarity.
- Julian Ceipek found an error and a number of typos.
- Stijn Debrouwere, Leo Marihart III, Jonathan Hammler, and Kent Johnson found errors in the first print edition.
- Dan Kearney found a typo.
- Jeff Pickhardt found a broken link and a typo.
- Jörg Beyer found typos in the book and made many corrections in the docstrings of the accompanying code.
- Tommie Gannert sent a patch file with a number of corrections.

Conventions Used in This Book

The following typographical conventions are used in this book:

Italic

> Indicates new terms, URLs, email addresses, filenames, and file extensions.

`Constant width`

> Used for program listings, as well as within paragraphs to refer to program elements such as variable or function names, databases, data types, environment variables, statements, and keywords.

`Constant width bold`

> Shows commands or other text that should be typed literally by the user.

`Constant width italic`

> Shows text that should be replaced with user-supplied values or by values determined by context.

 This icon signifies a tip, suggestion, or general note.

 This icon indicates a warning or caution.

Using Code Examples

This book is here to help you get your job done. In general, you may use the code in this book in your programs and documentation. You do not need to contact us for permission unless you're reproducing a significant portion of the code. For example, writing a program that uses several chunks of code from this book does not require permission. Selling or distributing a CD-ROM of examples from O'Reilly books does require permission. Answering a question by citing this book and quoting example code does not require permission. Incorporating a significant amount of example code from this book into your product's documentation does require permission.

We appreciate, but do not require, attribution. An attribution usually includes the title, author, publisher, and ISBN. For example: "*Think Stats* by Allen B. Downey (O'Reilly). Copyright 2011 Allen B. Downey, 978-1-449-30711-0."

If you feel your use of code examples falls outside fair use or the permission given above, feel free to contact us at *permissions@oreilly.com*.

Safari® Books Online

Safari Books Online is an on-demand digital library that lets you easily search over 7,500 technology and creative reference books and videos to find the answers you need quickly.

With a subscription, you can read any page and watch any video from our library online. Read books on your cell phone and mobile devices. Access new titles before they are available for print, and get exclusive access to manuscripts in development and post feedback for the authors. Copy and paste code samples, organize your favorites, download chapters, bookmark key sections, create notes, print out pages, and benefit from tons of other time-saving features.

O'Reilly Media has uploaded this book to the Safari Books Online service. To have full digital access to this book and others on similar topics from O'Reilly and other publishers, sign up for free at *http://my.safaribooksonline.com*.

How to Contact Us

Please address comments and questions concerning this book to the publisher:

O'Reilly Media, Inc.
1005 Gravenstein Highway North
Sebastopol, CA 95472
800-998-9938 (in the United States or Canada)
707-829-0515 (international or local)
707-829-0104 (fax)

We have a web page for this book, where we list errata, examples, and any additional information. You can access this page at:

http://www.oreilly.com/catalog/0636920020745

To comment or ask technical questions about this book, send email to:

bookquestions@oreilly.com

For more information about our books, courses, conferences, and news, see our website at *http://www.oreilly.com*.

Find us on Facebook: *http://facebook.com/oreilly*

Follow us on Twitter: *http://twitter.com/oreillymedia*

Watch us on YouTube: *http://www.youtube.com/oreillymedia*

CHAPTER 1

Statistical Thinking for Programmers

This book is about turning data into knowledge. Data is cheap (at least relatively); knowledge is harder to come by.

I will present three related pieces:

Probability
> The study of random events. Most people have an intuitive understanding of degrees of probability, which is why you can use words like "probably" and "unlikely" without special training, but we will talk about how to make quantitative claims about those degrees.

Statistics
> The discipline of using data samples to support claims about populations. Most statistical analysis is based on probability, which is why these pieces are usually presented together.

Computation
> A tool that is well-suited to quantitative analysis. Computers are commonly used to process statistics. Also, computational experiments are useful for exploring concepts in probability and statistics.

The thesis of this book is that if you know how to program, you can use that skill to help you understand probability and statistics. These topics are often presented from a mathematical perspective, and that approach works well for some people. But some important ideas in this area are hard to work with mathematically and relatively easy to approach computationally.

The rest of this chapter presents a case study motivated by a question I heard when my wife and I were expecting our first child: do first babies tend to arrive late?

Do First Babies Arrive Late?

If you Google this question, you will find plenty of discussion. Some people claim it's true, others say it's a myth, and some people say it's the other way around: first babies come early.

In many of these discussions, people provide data to support their claims. I found many examples like these:

> "My two friends that have given birth recently to their first babies, BOTH went almost 2 weeks overdue before going into labor or being induced."

> "My first one came 2 weeks late and now I think the second one is going to come out two weeks early!!"

> "I don't think that can be true because my sister was my mother's first and she was early, as with many of my cousins."

Reports like these are called *anecdotal evidence* because they are based on data that is unpublished and usually personal. In casual conversation, there is nothing wrong with anecdotes, so I don't mean to pick on the people I quoted.

But we might want evidence that is more persuasive and an answer that is more reliable. By those standards, anecdotal evidence usually fails, because:

Small number of observations
> If the gestation period is longer for first babies, the difference is probably small compared to the natural variation. In that case, we might have to compare a large number of pregnancies to be sure that a difference exists.

Selection bias
> People who join a discussion of this question might be interested because their first babies were late. In that case, the process of selecting data would bias the results.

Confirmation bias
> People who believe the claim might be more likely to contribute examples that confirm it. People who doubt the claim are more likely to cite counterexamples.

Inaccuracy
> Anecdotes are often personal stories, and often misremembered, misrepresented, repeated inaccurately, etc.

So how can we do better?

A Statistical Approach

To address the limitations of anecdotes, we will use the tools of statistics, which include:

Data collection
> We will use data from a large national survey that was designed explicitly with the goal of generating statistically valid inferences about the U.S. population.

Descriptive statistics
> We will generate statistics that summarize the data concisely, and evaluate different ways to visualize data.

Exploratory data analysis
> We will look for patterns, differences, and other features that address the questions we are interested in. At the same time, we will check for inconsistencies and identify limitations.

Hypothesis testing
> Where we see apparent effects, like a difference between two groups, we will evaluate whether the effect is real, or whether it might have happened by chance.

Estimation
> We will use data from a sample to estimate characteristics of the general population.

By performing these steps with care to avoid pitfalls, we can reach conclusions that are more justifiable and more likely to be correct.

The National Survey of Family Growth

Since 1973, the U.S. Centers for Disease Control and Prevention (CDC) have conducted the National Survey of Family Growth (NSFG), which is intended to gather "information on family life, marriage and divorce, pregnancy, infertility, use of contraception, and men's and women's health. The survey results are used ... to plan health services and health education programs, and to do statistical studies of families, fertility, and health."[1]

We will use data collected by this survey to investigate whether first babies tend to come late, and other questions. In order to use this data effectively, we have to understand the design of the study.

The NSFG is a *cross-sectional* study, which means that it captures a snapshot of a group at a point in time. The most common alternative is a *longitudinal* study, which observes a group repeatedly over a period of time.

The NSFG has been conducted seven times; each deployment is called a *cycle*. We will be using data from Cycle 6, which was conducted from January 2002 to March 2003.

---

1. See *http://cdc.gov/nchs/nsfg.htm*.

The goal of the survey is to draw conclusions about a *population*; the target population of the NSFG is people in the United States aged 15–44.

The people who participate in a survey are called *respondents*; a group of respondents is called a *cohort*. In general, cross-sectional studies are meant to be *representative*, which means that every member of the target population has an equal chance of participating. Of course, that ideal is hard to achieve in practice, but people who conduct surveys come as close as they can.

The NSFG is not representative; instead, it is deliberately *oversampled*. The designers of the study recruited three groups—Hispanics, African-Americans, and teenagers—at rates higher than their representation in the U.S. population. The reason for oversampling is to make sure that the number of respondents in each of these groups is large enough to draw valid statistical inferences.

Of course, the drawback of oversampling is that it is not as easy to draw conclusions about the general population based on statistics from the survey. We will come back to this point later.

Exercise 1-1.

Although the NSFG has been conducted seven times, it is not a longitudinal study. Read the Wikipedia pages *http://wikipedia.org/wiki/Cross-sectional_study* and *http:// wikipedia.org/wiki/Longitudinal_study* to make sure you understand why not.

Exercise 1-2.

In this exercise, you will download data from the NSFG; we will use this data throughout the book.

1. Go to *http://thinkstats.com/nsfg.html*. Read the terms of use for this data and click "I accept these terms" (assuming that you do).

2. Download the files named 2002FemResp.dat.gz and 2002FemPreg.dat.gz. The first is the respondent file, which contains one line for each of the 7,643 female respondents. The second file contains one line for each pregnancy reported by a respondent.

3. Online documentation of the survey is at *http://www.icpsr.umich.edu/nsfg6*. Browse the sections in the left navigation bar to get a sense of what data is included. You can also read the questionnaires at *http://cdc.gov/nchs/data/nsfg/nsfg_2002 _questionnaires.htm*.

4. The web page for this book provides code to process the data files from the NSFG. Download *http://thinkstats.com/survey.py* and run it in the same directory you put the data files in. It should read the data files and print the number of lines in each:

```
Number of respondents 7643
Number of pregnancies 13593
```

5. Browse the code to get a sense of what it does. The next section explains how it works.

Tables and Records

The poet-philosopher Steve Martin once said:

> "Oeuf" means egg, "chapeau" means hat. It's like those French have a different word for everything.

Like the French, database programmers speak a slightly different language, and since we're working with a database, we need to learn some vocabulary.

Each line in the respondents file contains information about one respondent. This information is called a *record*. The variables that make up a record are called *fields*. A collection of records is called a *table*.

If you read `survey.py`, you will see class definitions for `Record`, which is an object that represents a record, and `Table`, which represents a table.

There are two subclasses of `Record`—`Respondent` and `Pregnancy`—which contain records from the respondent and pregnancy tables. For the time being, these classes are empty; in particular, there is no init method to initialize their attributes. Instead, we will use `Table.MakeRecord` to convert a line of text into a `Record` object.

There are also two subclasses of `Table`: `Respondents` and `Pregnancies`. The init method in each class specifies the default name of the data file and the type of record to create. Each `Table` object has an attribute named `records`, which is a list of `Record` objects.

For each `Table`, the `GetFields` method returns a list of tuples that specify the fields from the record that will be stored as attributes in each `Record` object. (You might want to read that last sentence twice.)

For example, here is `Pregnancies.GetFields`:

```
def GetFields(self):
      return [
          ('caseid', 1, 12, int),
          ('prglength', 275, 276, int),
          ('outcome', 277, 277, int),
          ('birthord', 278, 279, int),
          ('finalwgt', 423, 440, float),
          ]
```

The first tuple says that the field `caseid` is in columns 1 through 12 and it's an integer. Each tuple contains the following information:

field
> The name of the attribute where the field will be stored. Most of the time, I use the name from the NSFG codebook, converted to all lowercase.

start
> The index of the starting column for this field. For example, the start index for `caseid` is 1. You can look up these indices in the NSFG codebook at *http://nsfg.icpsr .umich.edu/cocoon/WebDocs/NSFG/public/index.htm*.

end

The index of the ending column for this field; for example, the end index for `caseid` is 12. Unlike in Python, the end index is *inclusive*.

conversion function

A function that takes a string and converts it to an appropriate type. You can use built-in functions, like `int` and `float`, or user-defined functions. If the conversion fails, the attribute gets the string value `'NA'`. If you don't want to convert a field, you can provide an identity function or use `str`.

For pregnancy records, we extract the following variables:

caseid

The integer ID of the respondent.

prglength

The integer duration of the pregnancy in weeks.

outcome

An integer code for the outcome of the pregnancy. The code 1 indicates a live birth.

birthord

The integer birth order of each live birth; for example, the code for a first child is 1. For outcomes other than live birth, this field is blank.

finalwgt

The statistical weight associated with the respondent. It is a floating-point value that indicates the number of people in the U.S. population this respondent represents. Members of oversampled groups have lower weights.

If you read the casebook carefully, you will see that most of these variables are *recodes*, which means that they are not part of the *raw data* collected by the survey, but they are calculated using the raw data.

For example, `prglength` for live births is equal to the raw variable `wksgest` (weeks of gestation) if it is available; otherwise, it is estimated using `mosgest * 4.33` (months of gestation times the average number of weeks in a month).

Recodes are often based on logic that checks the consistency and accuracy of the data. In general it is a good idea to use recodes unless there is a compelling reason to process the raw data yourself.

You might also notice that `Pregnancies` has a method called `Recode` that does some additional checking and recoding.

Exercise 1-3.

In this exercise you will write a program to explore the data in the Pregnancies table.

1. In the directory where you put survey.py and the data files, create a file named first.py and type or paste in the following code:

```
import survey
table = survey.Pregnancies()
table.ReadRecords()
print 'Number of pregnancies', len(table.records)
```

The result should be 13,593 pregnancies.

2. Write a loop that iterates table and counts the number of live births. Find the documentation of outcome and confirm that your result is consistent with the summary in the documentation.

3. Modify the loop to partition the live birth records into two groups, one for first babies and one for the others. Again, read the documentation of birthord to see if your results are consistent.

When you are working with a new dataset, these kinds of checks are useful for finding errors and inconsistencies in the data, detecting bugs in your program, and checking your understanding of the way the fields are encoded.

4. Compute the average pregnancy length (in weeks) for first babies and others. Is there a difference between the groups? How big is it?

You can download a solution to this exercise from *http://thinkstats.com/first.py*.

Significance

In the previous exercise, you compared the gestation period for first babies and others; if things worked out, you found that first babies are born about 13 hours later, on average.

A difference like that is called an *apparent effect*; that is, there might be something going on, but we are not yet sure. There are several questions we still want to ask:

- If the two groups have different means, what about other *summary statistics*, like median and variance? Can we be more precise about how the groups differ?

- Is it possible that the difference we saw could occur by chance, even if the groups we compared were actually the same? If so, we would conclude that the effect was not *statistically significant*.

- Is it possible that the apparent effect is due to selection bias or some other error in the experimental setup? If so, then we might conclude that the effect is an *artifact*; that is, something we created (by accident) rather than found.

Answering these questions will take most of the rest of this book.

Exercise 1-4.

The best way to learn about statistics is to work on a project you are interested in. Is there a question like, "Do first babies arrive late," that you would like to investigate?

Think about questions you find personally interesting, items of conventional wisdom, controversial topics, or questions that have political consequences, and see if you can formulate a question that lends itself to statistical inquiry.

Look for data to help you address the question. Governments are good sources because data from public research is often freely available.[2] Another way to find data is Wolfram Alpha, which is a curated collection of good-quality datasets at *http://wolframalpha .com*. Results from Wolfram Alpha are subject to copyright restrictions; you might want to check the terms before you commit yourself.

Google and other search engines can also help you find data, but it can be harder to evaluate the quality of resources on the web.

If it seems like someone has answered your question, look closely to see whether the answer is justified. There might be flaws in the data or the analysis that make the conclusion unreliable. In that case, you could perform a different analysis of the same data, or look for a better source of data.

If you find a published paper that addresses your question, you should be able to get the raw data. Many authors make their data available on the web, but for sensitive data you might have to write to the authors, provide information about how you plan to use the data, or agree to certain terms of use. Be persistent!

Glossary

anecdotal evidence
> Evidence, often personal, that is collected casually rather than by a well-designed study.

apparent effect
> A measurement or summary statistic that suggests that something interesting is happening.

artifact
> An apparent effect that is caused by bias, measurement error, or some other kind of error.

cohort
> A group of respondents.

cross-sectional study
> A study that collects data about a population at a particular point in time.

---

2. On the day I wrote this paragraph, a court in the UK ruled that the Freedom of Information Act applies to scientific research data.

field
> In a database, one of the named variables that makes up a record.

longitudinal study
> A study that follows a population over time, collecting data from the same group repeatedly.

oversampling
> The technique of increasing the representation of a sub-population in order to avoid errors due to small sample sizes.

population
> A group we are interested in studying, often a group of people, but the term is also used for animals, vegetables, and minerals.[3]

raw data
> Values collected and recorded with little or no checking, calculation, or interpretation.

recode
> A value that is generated by calculation and other logic applied to raw data.

record
> In a database, a collection of information about a single person or other object of study.

representative
> A sample is representative if every member of the population has the same chance of being in the sample.

respondent
> A person who responds to a survey.

sample
> The subset of a population used to collect data.

statistically significant
> An apparent effect is statistically significant if it is unlikely to occur by chance.

summary statistic:
> The result of a computation that reduces a dataset to a single number (or at least a smaller set of numbers) that captures some characteristic of the data.

table
> In a database, a collection of records.

---

3. If you don't recognize this phrase, see *http://wikipedia.org/wiki/Twenty_Questions*.

CHAPTER 2

Descriptive Statistics

Means and Averages

In the previous chapter, I mentioned three summary statistics—mean, variance, and median—without explaining what they are. So before we go any farther, let's take care of that.

If you have a sample of n values, x_i, the mean, μ, is the sum of the values divided by the number of values; in other words

$$\mu = \frac{1}{n} \sum_i x_i$$

The words "mean" and "average" are sometimes used interchangeably, but I will maintain this distinction:

- The "mean" of a sample is the summary statistic computed with the previous formula.
- An "average" is one of many summary statistics you might choose to describe the typical value or the *central tendency* of a sample.

Sometimes the mean is a good description of a set of values. For example, apples are all pretty much the same size (at least the ones sold in supermarkets). So if I buy six apples and the total weight is three pounds, it would be reasonable to conclude that they are about a half pound each.

But pumpkins are more diverse. Suppose I grow several varieties in my garden, and one day I harvest three decorative pumpkins that are one pound each, two pie pumpkins that are three pounds each, and one Atlantic Giant pumpkin that weighs 591 pounds. The mean of this sample is 100 pounds, but if I told you "The average pumpkin in my garden is 100 pounds," that would be wrong, or at least misleading.

In this example, there is no meaningful average because there is no typical pumpkin.

Variance

If there is no single number that summarizes pumpkin weights, we can do a little better with two numbers: mean and *variance*.

In the same way that the mean is intended to describe the central tendency, variance is intended to describe the *spread*. The variance of a set of values is

$$\sigma^2 = \frac{1}{n} \sum_i (x_i - \mu)^2$$

The term x_i-μ is called the "deviation from the mean," so variance is the mean squared deviation, which is why it is denoted σ^2. The square root of variance, σ, is called the *standard deviation*.

By itself, variance is hard to interpret. One problem is that the units are strange; in this case, the measurements are in pounds, so the variance is in pounds squared. Standard deviation is more meaningful; in this case, the units are pounds.

Exercise 2-1.

For the exercises in this chapter, download *http://thinkstats.com/thinkstats.py*, which contains general-purpose functions we will use throughout the book. You can read documentation of these functions in *http://thinkstats.com/thinkstats.html*.

Write a function called `Pumpkin` that uses functions from `thinkstats.py` to compute the mean, variance, and standard deviation of the pumpkins weights in the previous section.

Exercise 2-2.

Reusing code from `survey.py` and `first.py`, compute the standard deviation of gestation time for first babies and others. Does it look like the spread is the same for the two groups?

How big is the difference in the means compared to these standard deviations? What does this comparison suggest about the statistical significance of the difference?

If you have prior experience, you might have seen a formula for variance with $n - 1$ in the denominator, rather than n. This statistic is called the "sample variance," and it is used to estimate the variance in a population using a sample. We will come back to this in Chapter 8.

Distributions

Summary statistics are concise, but dangerous, because they obscure the data. An alternative is to look at the *distribution* of the data, which describes how often each value appears.

The most common representation of a distribution is a *histogram*, which is a graph that shows the frequency or probability of each value.

In this context, *frequency* means the number of times a value appears in a dataset—it has nothing to do with the pitch of a sound or tuning of a radio signal. A *probability* is a frequency expressed as a fraction of the sample size, *n*.

In Python, an efficient way to compute frequencies is with a dictionary. Given a sequence of values, t:

```
hist = {}
for x in t:
    hist[x] = hist.get(x, 0) + 1
```

The result is a dictionary that maps from values to frequencies. To get from frequencies to probabilities, we divide through by *n*, which is called *normalization*:

```
n = float(len(t))
pmf = {}
for x, freq in hist.items():
    pmf[x] = freq / n
```

The normalized histogram is called a *PMF*, which stands for "probability mass function"; that is, it's a function that maps from values to probabilities (I'll explain "mass" in Exercise 6-5).

It might be confusing to call a Python dictionary a function. In mathematics, a function is a map from one set of values to another. In Python, we *usually* represent mathematical functions with function objects, but in this case we are using a dictionary (dictionaries are also called "maps," if that helps).

Representing Histograms

I wrote a Python module called Pmf.py that contains class definitions for Hist objects, which represent histograms, and Pmf objects, which represent PMFs. You can read the documentation at *http://thinkstats.com/Pmf.html* and download the code from *http://thinkstats.com/Pmf.py*.

The function MakeHistFromList takes a list of values and returns a new Hist object. You can test it in Python's interactive mode:

```
>>> import Pmf
>>> hist = Pmf.MakeHistFromList([1, 2, 2, 3, 5])
>>> print hist
<Pmf.Hist object at 0xb76cf68c>
```

Pmf.Hist means that this object is a member of the Hist class, which is defined in the Pmf module. In general, I use uppercase letters for the names of classes and functions, and lowercase letters for variables.

Hist objects provide methods to look up values and their probabilities. Freq takes a value and returns its frequency:

```
>>> hist.Freq(2)
2
```

If you look up a value that has never appeared, the frequency is 0.

```
>>> hist.Freq(4)
0
```

Values returns an unsorted list of the values in the Hist:

```
>>> hist.Values()
[1, 5, 3, 2]
```

To loop through the values in order, you can use the built-in function sorted:

```
for val in sorted(hist.Values()):
    print val, hist.Freq(val)
```

If you are planning to look up all of the frequencies, it is more efficient to use Items, which returns an unsorted list of value-frequency pairs:

```
for val, freq in hist.Items():
    print val, freq
```

Exercise 2-3.

The mode of a distribution is the most frequent value (see *http://wikipedia.org/wiki/ Mode_(statistics)*). Write a function called Mode that takes a Hist object and returns the most frequent value.

As a more challenging version, write a function called AllModes that takes a Hist object and returns a list of value-frequency pairs in descending order of frequency. Hint: the operator module provides a function called itemgetter which you can pass as a key to sorted.

Plotting Histograms

There are a number of Python packages for making figures and graphs. The one I will demonstrate is pyplot, which is part of the matplotlib package at *http://matplotlib.sour ceforge.net*.

This package is included in many Python installations. To see whether you have it, launch the Python interpreter and run:

```
import matplotlib.pyplot as pyplot
pyplot.pie([1,2,3])
pyplot.show()
```

If you have matplotlib you should see a simple pie chart; otherwise, you will have to install it.

Histograms and PMFs are most often plotted as bar charts. The pyplot function to draw a bar chart is bar. Hist objects provide a method called Render that returns a sorted list of values and a list of the corresponding frequencies, which is the format bar expects:

```
>>> vals, freqs = hist.Render()
>>> rectangles = pyplot.bar(vals, freqs)
>>> pyplot.show()
```

I wrote a module called myplot.py that provides functions for plotting histograms, PMFs, and other objects we will see soon. You can read the documentation at think stats.com/myplot.html and download the code from thinkstats.com/myplot.py. Or you can use pyplot directly, if you prefer. Either way, you can find the documentation for pyplot on the web.

Figure 2-1 shows histograms of pregnancy lengths for first babies and others.

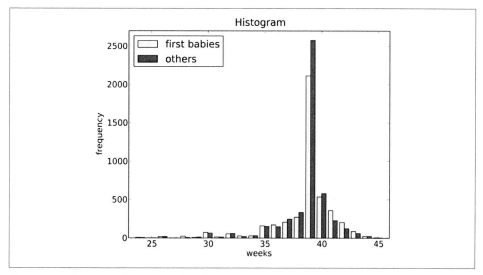

Figure 2-1. Histogram of pregnancy lengths

Histograms are useful because they make the following features immediately apparent:

Mode
    The most common value in a distribution is called the *mode*. In Figure 2-1, there is a clear mode at 39 weeks. In this case, the mode is the summary statistic that does the best job of describing the typical value.

Shape
    Around the mode, the distribution is asymmetric; it drops off quickly to the right and more slowly to the left. From a medical point of view, this makes sense. Babies are often born early, but seldom later than 42 weeks. Also, the right side of the distribution is truncated because doctors often intervene after 42 weeks.

Outliers
    Values far from the mode are called *outliers*. Some of these are just unusual cases, like babies born at 30 weeks. But many of them are probably due to errors, either in the reporting or recording of data.

Although histograms make some features apparent, they are usually not useful for comparing two distributions. In this example, there are fewer "first babies" than "others," so some of the apparent differences in the histograms are due to sample sizes. We can address this problem using PMFs.

Representing PMFs

`Pmf.py` provides a class called `Pmf` that represents PMFs. The notation can be confusing, but here it is: `Pmf` is the name of the module and also the class, so the full name of the class is `Pmf.Pmf`. I often use `pmf` as a variable name. Finally, in the text, I use PMF to refer to the general concept of a probability mass function, independent of my implementation.

To create a Pmf object, use `MakePmfFromList`, which takes a list of values:

```
>>> import Pmf
>>> pmf = Pmf.MakePmfFromList([1, 2, 2, 3, 5])
>>> print pmf
<Pmf.Pmf object at 0xb76cf68c>
```

Pmf and Hist objects are similar in many ways. The methods `Values` and `Items` work the same way for both types. The biggest difference is that a Hist maps from values to integer counters; a Pmf maps from values to floating-point probabilities.

To look up the probability associated with a value, use `Prob`:

```
>>> pmf.Prob(2)
0.4
```

You can modify an existing Pmf by incrementing the probability associated with a value:

```
>>> pmf.Incr(2, 0.2)
>>> pmf.Prob(2)
0.6
```

Or you can multiple a probability by a factor:

```
>>> pmf.Mult(2, 0.5)
>>> pmf.Prob(2)
0.3
```

If you modify a Pmf, the result may not be normalized; that is, the probabilities may no longer add up to 1. To check, you can call `Total`, which returns the sum of the probabilities:

```
>>> pmf.Total()
0.9
```

To renormalize, call `Normalize`:

```
>>> pmf.Normalize()
>>> pmf.Total()
1.0
```

Pmf objects provide a `Copy` method so you can make and and modify a copy without affecting the original.

Exercise 2-4.

According to Wikipedia, "Survival analysis is a branch of statistics which deals with death in biological organisms and failure in mechanical systems;" see *http://wikipedia.org/wiki/Survival_analysis*.

As part of survival analysis, it is often useful to compute the remaining lifetime of, for example, a mechanical component. If we know the distribution of lifetimes and the age of the component, we can compute the distribution of remaining lifetimes.

Write a function called `RemainingLifetime` that takes a Pmf of lifetimes and an age, and returns a new Pmf that represents the distribution of remaining lifetimes.

Exercise 2-5.

In "Means and Averages" on page 11 we computed the mean of a sample by adding up the elements and dividing by *n*. If you are given a PMF, you can still compute the mean, but the process is slightly different:

$$\mu = \sum_i p_i x_i$$

where the x_i are the unique values in the PMF and p_i=PMF(x_i). Similarly, you can compute variance like this:

$$\sigma^2 = \sum_i p_i (x_i - \mu)^2$$

Write functions called `PmfMean` and `PmfVar` that take a Pmf object and compute the mean and variance. To test these methods, check that they are consistent with the methods `Mean` and `Var` in `Pmf.py`.

Plotting PMFs

There are two common ways to plot Pmfs:

- To plot a Pmf as a bar graph, you can use `pyplot.bar` or `myplot.Hist`. Bar graphs are most useful if the number of values in the Pmf is small.
- To plot a Pmf as a line, you can use `pyplot.plot` or `myplot.Pmf`. Line plots are most useful if there are a large number of values and the Pmf is smooth.

Figure 2-2 shows the PMF of pregnancy lengths as a bar graph. Using the PMF, we can see more clearly where the distributions differ. First babies seem to be less likely to arrive on time (week 39) and more likely to be late (weeks 41 and 42).

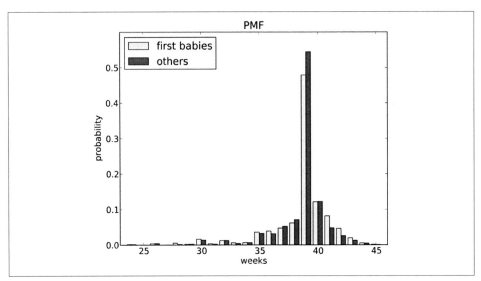

Figure 2-2. PMF of pregnancy lengths

The code that generates the figures in this chapters is available from *http://thinkstats .com/descriptive.py*. To run it, you will need the modules it imports and the data from the NSFG (see "The National Survey of Family Growth" on page 3).

Note: `pyplot` provides a function called `hist` that takes a sequence of values, computes the histogram, and plots it. Since I use `Hist` objects, I usually don't use `pyplot.hist`.

Outliers

Outliers are values that are far from the central tendency. Outliers might be caused by errors in collecting or processing the data, or they might be correct but unusual measurements. It is always a good idea to check for outliers, and sometimes it is useful and appropriate to discard them.

In the list of pregnancy lengths for live births, the ten lowest values are {0, 4, 9, 13, 17, 17, 18, 19, 20, 21}. Values below 20 weeks are certainly errors, and values higher than 30 weeks are probably legitimate. But values in between are hard to interpret.

On the other end, the highest values are:

```
weeks   count
 43      148
 44       46
 45       10
 46        1
 47        1
 48        7
 50        2
```

Again, some values are almost certainly errors, but it is hard to know for sure. One option is to *trim* the data by discarding some fraction of the highest and lowest values (see *http://wikipedia.org/wiki/Truncated_mean*).

Other Visualizations

Histograms and PMFs are useful for exploratory data analysis; once you have an idea of what is going on, it is often useful to design a visualization that focuses on the apparent effect.

In the NSFG data, the biggest differences in the distributions are near the mode. So it makes sense to zoom in on that part of the graph, and to transform the data to emphasize differences.

Figure 2-3 shows the difference between the PMFs for weeks 35–45. I multiplied by 100 to express the differences in percentage points.

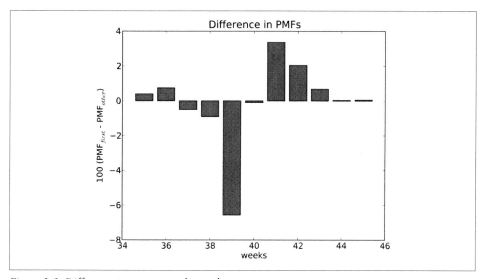

Figure 2-3. Difference in percentage, by week

This figure makes the pattern clearer: first babies are less likely to be born in week 39, and somewhat more likely to be born in weeks 41 and 42.

Relative Risk

We started with the question, "Do first babies arrive late?" To make that more precise, let's say that a baby is early if it is born during Week 37 or earlier, on time if it is born during Week 38, 39, or 40, and late if it is born during Week 41 or later. Ranges like these that are used to group data are called *bins*.

Exercise 2-6.

Create a file named `risk.py`. Write functions named `ProbEarly`, `ProbOnTime`, and `ProbLate` that take a PMF and compute the fraction of births that fall into each bin. Hint: write a generalized function that these functions call.

Make three PMFs, one for first babies, one for others, and one for all live births. For each PMF, compute the probability of being born early, on time, or late.

One way to summarize data like this is with *relative risk*, which is a ratio of two probabilities. For example, the probability that a first baby is born early is 18.2%. For other babies it is 16.8%, so the relative risk is 1.08. That means that first babies are about 8% more likely to be early.

Write code to confirm that result, then compute the relative risks of being born on time and being late. You can download a solution from *http://thinkstats.com/risk.py*.

Conditional Probability

Imagine that someone you know is pregnant, and it is the beginning of Week 39. What is the chance that the baby will be born in the next week? How much does the answer change if it's a first baby?

We can answer these questions by computing a *conditional probability*, which is (ahem!) a probability that depends on a condition. In this case, the condition is that we know the baby didn't arrive during Weeks 0–38.

Here's one way to do it:

1. Given a PMF, generate a fake cohort of 1,000 pregnancies. For each number of weeks, x, the number of pregnancies with duration x is 1,000 PMF(x).

2. Remove from the cohort all pregnancies with length less than 39.

3. Compute the PMF of the remaining durations; the result is the conditional PMF.

4. Evaluate the conditional PMF at $x = 39$ weeks.

This algorithm is conceptually clear, but not very efficient. A simple alternative is to remove from the distribution the values less than 39 and then renormalize.

Exercise 2-7.

Write a function that implements either of these algorithms and computes the probability that a baby will be born during Week 39, given that it was not born prior to Week 39.

Generalize the function to compute the probability that a baby will be born during Week x, given that it was not born prior to Week x, for all x. Plot this value as a function of x for first babies and others.

You can download a solution to this problem from *http://thinkstats.com/conditional.py*.

Reporting Results

At this point, we have explored the data and seen several apparent effects. For now, let's assume that these effects are real (but let's remember that it's an assumption). How should we report these results?

The answer might depend on who is asking the question. For example, a scientist might be interested in any (real) effect, no matter how small. A doctor might only care about effects that are *clinically significant*; that is, differences that affect treatment decisions. A pregnant woman might be interested in results that are relevant to her, like the conditional probabilities in the previous section.

How you report results also depends on your goals. If you are trying to demonstrate the significance of an effect, you might choose summary statistics, like relative risk, that emphasize differences. If you are trying to reassure a patient, you might choose statistics that put the differences in context.

Exercise 2-8.

Based on the results from the previous exercises, suppose you were asked to summarize what you learned about whether first babies arrive late.

Which summary statistics would you use if you wanted to get a story on the evening news? Which ones would you use if you wanted to reassure an anxious patient?

Finally, imagine that you are Cecil Adams, author of *The Straight Dope* (*http://straight dope.com*), and your job is to answer the question, "Do first babies arrive late?" Write a paragraph that uses the results in this chapter to answer the question clearly, precisely, and accurately.

Glossary

bin
    A range used to group nearby values.

central tendency
    A characteristic of a sample or population; intuitively, it is the most average value.

clinically significant
    A result, like a difference between groups, that is relevant in practice.

conditional probability
    A probability computed under the assumption that some condition holds.

distribution
    A summary of the values that appear in a sample and the frequency, or probability, of each.

frequency
    The number of times a value appears in a sample.

histogram
> A mapping from values to frequencies, or a graph that shows this mapping.

mode
> The most frequent value in a sample.

normalization
> The process of dividing a frequency by a sample size to get a probability.

outlier
> A value far from the central tendency.

probability
> A frequency expressed as a fraction of the sample size.

probability mass function (PMF)
> A representation of a distribution as a function that maps from values to probabilities.

relative risk
> A ratio of two probabilities, often used to measure a difference between distributions.

spread
> A characteristic of a sample or population; intuitively, it describes how much variability there is.

standard deviation
> The square root of variance, also used as a measure of spread.

trim
> To remove outliers from a dataset.

variance
> A summary statistic often used to quantify spread.

CHAPTER 3

Cumulative Distribution Functions

The Class Size Paradox

At many American colleges and universities, the student-to-faculty ratio is about 10:1. But students are often surprised to discover that their average class size is bigger than 10. There are two reasons for the discrepancy:

- Students typically take 4–5 classes per semester, but professors often teach 1 or 2.
- The number of students who enjoy a small class is small, but the number of students in a large class is (ahem!) large.

The first effect is obvious (at least once it is pointed out); the second is more subtle. So let's look at an example. Suppose that a college offers 65 classes in a given semester, with the following distribution of sizes:

```
size     count
5-9        8
10-14      8
15-19     14
20-24      4
25-29      6
30-34     12
35-39      8
40-44      3
45-49      2
```

If you ask the Dean for the average class size, he would construct a PMF, compute the mean, and report that the average class size is 24.

But if you survey a group of students, ask them how many students are in their classes, and compute the mean, you would think that the average class size was higher.

Exercise 3-1.

Build a PMF of these data and compute the mean as perceived by the Dean. Since the data have been grouped in bins, you can use the mid-point of each bin.

Now find the distribution of class sizes as perceived by students and compute its mean.

Suppose you want to find the distribution of class sizes at a college, but you can't get reliable data from the Dean. An alternative is to choose a random sample of students and ask them the number of students in each of their classes. Then you could compute the PMF of their responses.

The result would be biased because large classes would be oversampled, but you could estimate the actual distribution of class sizes by applying an appropriate transformation to the observed distribution.

Write a function called `UnbiasPmf` that takes the PMF of the observed values and returns a new Pmf object that estimates the distribution of class sizes.

You can download a solution to this problem from *http://thinkstats.com/class_size.py*.

Exercise 3-2.

In most foot races, everyone starts at the same time. If you are a fast runner, you usually pass a lot of people at the beginning of the race, but after a few miles everyone around you is going at the same speed.

When I ran a long-distance (209 miles) relay race for the first time, I noticed an odd phenomenon: when I overtook another runner, I was usually much faster, and when another runner overtook me, he was usually much faster.

At first I thought that the distribution of speeds might be bimodal; that is, there were many slow runners and many fast runners, but few at my speed.

Then I realized that I was the victim of selection bias. The race was unusual in two ways: it used a staggered start, so teams started at different times; also, many teams included runners at different levels of ability.

As a result, runners were spread out along the course with little relationship between speed and location. When I started running my leg, the runners near me were (pretty much) a random sample of the runners in the race.

So where does the bias come from? During my time on the course, the chance of over-taking a runner, or being overtaken, is proportional to the difference in our speeds. To see why, think about the extremes. If another runner is going at the same speed as me, neither of us will overtake the other. If someone is going so fast that they cover the entire course while I am running, they are certain to overtake me.

Write a function called `BiasPmf` that takes a Pmf representing the actual distribution of runners' speeds, and the speed of a running observer, and returns a new Pmf representing the distribution of runners' speeds as seen by the observer.

To test your function, get the distribution of speeds from a normal road race (not a relay). I wrote a program that reads the results from the James Joyce Ramble 10K in Dedham, MA, and converts the pace of each runner to mph. Download it from *http://thinkstats.com/relay.py*. Run it and look at the PMF of speeds.

Now compute the distribution of speeds you would observe if you ran a relay race at 7.5 mph with this group of runners. You can download a solution from *http://thinkstats.com/relay_soln.py*.

The Limits of PMFs

PMFs work well if the number of values is small. But as the number of values increases, the probability associated with each value gets smaller and the effect of random noise increases.

For example, we might be interested in the distribution of birth weights. In the NSFG data, the variable `totalwgt_oz` records weight at birth in ounces. Figure 3-1 shows the PMF of these values for first babies and others; it also illustrates a limitation of PMFs: they are hard to compare.

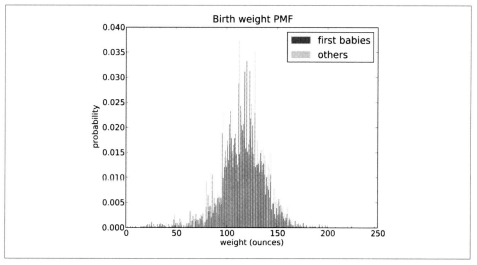

Figure 3-1. PMF of birth weights

Overall, these distributions resemble the familiar "bell curve," with many values near the mean and a few values much higher and lower.

But parts of this figure are hard to interpret. There are many spikes and valleys, and some apparent differences between the distributions. It is hard to tell which of these features are significant. Also, it is hard to see overall patterns; for example, which distribution do you think has the higher mean?

These problems can be mitigated by binning the data; that is, dividing the domain into non-overlapping intervals and counting the number of values in each bin. Binning can be useful, but it is tricky to get the size of the bins right. If they are big enough to smooth out noise, they might also smooth out useful information.

An alternative that avoids these problems is the *cumulative distribution function*, or CDF. But before we can get to that, we have to talk about percentiles.

Percentiles

If you have taken a standardized test, you probably got your results in the form of a raw score and a *percentile rank*. In this context, the percentile rank is the fraction of people who scored lower than you (or the same). So if you are "in the 90th percentile," you did as well as or better than 90% of the people who took the exam.

Here's how you could compute the percentile rank of a value, your_score, relative to the scores in the sequence scores:

```
def PercentileRank(scores, your_score):
    count = 0
    for score in scores:
        if score <= your_score:
            count += 1

    percentile_rank = 100.0 * count / len(scores)
    return percentile_rank
```

For example, if the scores in the sequence were 55, 66, 77, 88, and 99, and you got the 88, then your percentile rank would be 100 * 4 / 5 which is 80.

If you are given a value, it is easy to find its percentile rank; going the other way is slightly harder. If you are given a percentile rank and you want to find the corresponding value, one option is to sort the values and search for the one you want:

```
def Percentile(scores, percentile_rank):
    scores.sort()
    for score in scores:
        if PercentileRank(scores, score) >= percentile_rank:
            return score
```

The result of this calculation is a *percentile*. For example, the 50th percentile is the value with percentile rank 50. In the distribution of exam scores, the 50th percentile is 77.

Exercise 3-3.

This implementation of Percentile is not very efficient. A better approach is to use the percentile rank to compute the index of the corresponding percentile. Write a version of Percentile that uses this algorithm.

You can download a solution from *http://thinkstats.com/score_example.py*.

Exercise 3-4.

Optional: If you only want to compute one percentile, it is not efficient to sort the scores. A better option is the selection algorithm, which you can read about at *http://wikipedia.org/wiki/Selection_algorithm*.

Write (or find) an implementation of the selection algorithm and use it to write an efficient version of `Percentile`.

Cumulative Distribution Functions

Now that we understand percentiles, we are ready to tackle the cumulative distribution function (CDF). The CDF is the function that maps values to their percentile rank in a distribution.

The CDF is a function of x, where x is any value that might appear in the distribution. To evaluate CDF(x) for a particular value of x, we compute the fraction of the values in the sample less than (or equal to) x.

Here's what that looks like as a function that takes a sample, t, and a value, x:

```
def Cdf(t, x):
    count = 0.0
    for value in t:
        if value <= x:
            count += 1.0

    prob = count / len(t)
    return prob
```

This function should look familiar; it is almost identical to `PercentileRank`, except that the result is in a probability in the range 0–1 rather than a percentile rank in the range 0–100.

As an example, suppose a sample has the values {1, 2, 2, 3, 5}. Here are some values from its CDF:

CDF(0) = 0
CDF(1) = 0.2
CDF(2) = 0.6
CDF(3) = 0.8
CDF(4) = 0.8
CDF(5) = 1

We can evaluate the CDF for any value of x, not just values that appear in the sample. If x is less than the smallest value in the sample, CDF(x) is 0. If x is greater than the largest value, CDF(x) is 1.

Figure 3-2 is a graphical representation of this CDF. The CDF of a sample is a step function. In the next chapter, we will see distributions whose CDFs are continuous functions.

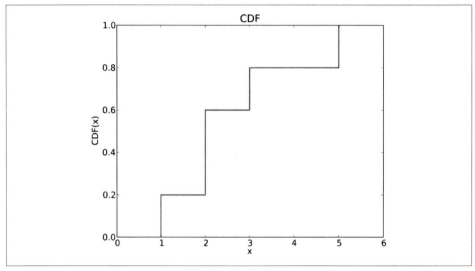

Figure 3-2. Example of a CDF

Representing CDFs

I have written a module called Cdf that provides a class named Cdf that represents CDFs. You can read the documentation of this module at *http://thinkstats.com/Cdf.html* and you can download it from *http://thinkstats.com/Cdf.py*.

Cdfs are implemented with two sorted lists: xs, which contains the values, and ps, which contains the probabilities. The most important methods Cdfs provide are:

Prob(x):
    Given a value *x*, computes the probability *p* = CDF(*x*).

Value(p):
    Given a probability *p*, computes the corresponding value, *x*; that is, the inverse CDF of *p*.

Because xs and ps are sorted, these operations can use the bisection algorithm, which is efficient. The run time is proportional to the logarithm of the number of values; see *http://wikipedia.org/wiki/Time_complexity*.

Cdfs also provide `Render`, which returns two lists, `xs` and `ps`, suitable for plotting the CDF. Because the CDF is a step function, these lists have two elements for each unique value in the distribution.

The Cdf module provides several functions for making Cdfs, including `MakeCdfFromList`, which takes a sequence of values and returns their Cdf.

Finally, `myplot.py` provides functions named `Cdf` and `Cdfs` that plot Cdfs as lines.

Exercise 3-5.

Download `Cdf.py` and `relay.py` (see Exercise 3-2) and generate a plot that shows the CDF of running speeds. Which gives you a better sense of the shape of the distribution, the PMF or the CDF? You can download a solution from *http://thinkstats.com/relay_cdf .py.*

Back to the Survey Data

Figure 3-3 shows the CDFs of birth weight for first babies and others in the NSFG dataset.

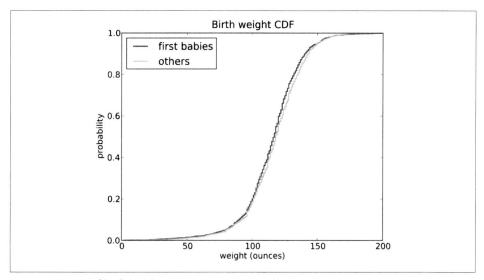

Figure 3-3. CDF of birth weights

This figure makes the shape of the distributions, and the differences between them, much clearer. We can see that first babies are slightly lighter throughout the distribution, with a larger discrepancy above the mean.

Exercise 3-6.

How much did you weigh at birth? If you don't know, call your mother or someone else who knows. Using the pooled data (all live births), compute the distribution of birth weights and use it to find your percentile rank. If you were a first baby, find your percentile rank in the distribution for first babies. Otherwise, use the distribution for others. How big is the difference between your percentile ranks in the two distributions?

Exercise 3-7.

Suppose you and your classmates compute the percentile rank of your birth weights and then compute the CDF of the percentile ranks. What do you expect it to look like? Hint: what fraction of the class do you expect to be above the median?

Conditional Distributions

A *conditional distribution* is the distribution of a subset of the data which is selected according to a condition.

For example, if you are above average in weight, but way above average in height, then you might be relatively light for your height. Here's how you could make that claim more precise.

1. Select a cohort of people who are the same height as you (within some range).
2. Find the CDF of weight for those people.
3. Find the percentile rank of your weight in that distribution.

Percentile ranks are useful for comparing measurements from different tests, or tests applied to different groups.

For example, people who compete in foot races are usually grouped by age and gender. To compare people in different groups, you can convert race times to percentile ranks.

Exercise 3-8.

I recently ran the James Joyce Ramble 10K in Dedham, MA. The results are available from *http://coolrunning.com/results/10/ma/Apr25_27thAn_set1.shtml*. Go to that page and find my results. I came in 97th in a field of 1,633, so what is my percentile rank in the field?

In my division (M4049 means "male between 40 and 49 years of age") I came in 26th out of 256. What is my percentile rank in my division?

If I am still running in 10 years (and I hope I am), I will be in the M5059 division. Assuming that my percentile rank in my division is the same, how much slower should I expect to be?

I maintain a friendly rivalry with a student of mine who is in the F2029 division. How fast does she have to run her next 10K to "beat" me in terms of percentile ranks?

Random Numbers

CDFs are useful for generating random numbers with a given distribution. Here's how:

- Choose a random probability in the range 0–1.
- Use `Cdf.Value` to find the value in the distribution that corresponds to the probability you chose.

It might not be obvious why this works, but since it is easier to implement than to explain, let's try it out.

Exercise 3-9.

Write a function called `Sample`, that takes a Cdf and an integer, *n*, and returns a list of *n* values chosen at random from the Cdf. Hint: use `random.random`. You will find a solution to this exercise in `Cdf.py`.

Using the distribution of birth weights from the NSFG, generate a random sample with 1,000 elements. Compute the CDF of the sample. Make a plot that shows the original CDF and the CDF of the random sample. For large values of *n*, the distributions should be the same.

This process, generating a random sample based on a measured sample, is called *resampling*.

There are two ways to draw a sample from a population: with and without replacement. If you imagine drawing marbles from an urn,[1] "replacement" means putting the marbles back as you go (and stirring), so the population is the same for every draw. "Without replacement," means that each marble can only be drawn once, so the remaining population is different after each draw.

In Python, sampling with replacement can be implemented with `random.random` to choose a percentile rank, or `random.choice` to choose an element from a sequence. Sampling without replacement is provided by `random.sample`.

Exercise 3-10.

The numbers generated by `random.random` are supposed to be uniform between 0 and 1; that is, every value in the range should have the same probability.

Generate 1,000 numbers from `random.random` and plot their PMF and CDF. Can you tell whether they are uniform?

You can read about the uniform distribution at *http://wikipedia.org/wiki/Uniform_dis tribution_(discrete)*.

---

1. The marbles-in-an-urn scenario is a standard model for random sampling processes (see *http://wikipedia .org/wiki/Urn_problem*).

Summary Statistics Revisited

Once you have computed a CDF, it is easy to compute other summary statistics. The median is just the 50th percentile.[2] The 25th and 75th percentiles are often used to check whether a distribution is symmetric, and their difference, which is called the *interquartile range*, measures the spread.

Exercise 3-11.

Write a function called Median that takes a Cdf and computes the median, and one called Interquartile that computes the interquartile range.

Compute the 25th, 50th, and 75th percentiles of the birth weight CDF. Do these values suggest that the distribution is symmetric?

Glossary

conditional distribution
    A distribution computed under the assumption that some condition holds.
cumulative distribution function (CDF)
    A function that maps from values to their percentile ranks.
interquartile range
    A measure of spread, the difference between the 75th and 25th percentiles.
percentile
    The value associated with a given percentile rank.
percentile rank
    The percentage of values in a distribution that are less than or equal to a given value.
replacement
    During a sampling process, "replacement" indicates that the population is the same for every sample. "Without replacement" indicates that each element can be selected only once.
resampling
    The process of generating a random sample from a distribution that was computed from a sample.

---

2. You might see other definitions of the median. In particular, some sources suggest that if you have an even number of elements in a sample, the median is the average of the middle two elements. This is an unnecessary special case, and it has the odd effect of generating a value that is not in the sample. As far as I'm concerned, the median is the 50th percentile. Period.

CHAPTER 4

Continuous Distributions

The distributions we have used so far are called *empirical distributions* because they are based on empirical observations, which are necessarily finite samples.

The alternative is a *continuous distribution*, which is characterized by a CDF that is a continuous function (as opposed to a step function). Many real-world phenomena can be approximated by continuous distributions.

The Exponential Distribution

I'll start with the exponential distribution because it is easy to work with. In the real world, exponential distributions come up when we look at a series of events and measure the times between events, which are called *interarrival times*. If the events are equally likely to occur at any time, the distribution of interarrival times tends to look like an exponential distribution.

The CDF of the exponential distribution is:

$$CDF(x) = 1 - e^{-\lambda x}$$

The parameter, λ, determines the shape of the distribution. Figure 4-1 shows what this CDF looks like with $\lambda = 2$.

In general, the mean of an exponential distribution is $1/\lambda$, so the mean of this distribution is 0.5. The median is $\log(2)/\lambda$, which is roughly 0.35.

To see an example of a distribution that is approximately exponential, we will look at the interarrival time of babies. On December 18, 1997, 44 babies were born in a hospital in Brisbane, Australia.[1] The times of birth for all 44 babies were reported in the local paper; you can download the data from *http://thinkstats.com/babyboom.dat*.

---

1. This example is based on information and data from Dunn, "A Simple Dataset for Demonstrating Common Distributions," Journal of Statistics Education v.7, n.3 (1999).

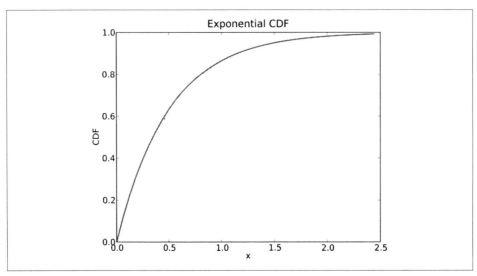

Figure 4-1. CDF of exponential distribution

Figure 4-2 shows the CDF of the interarrival times in minutes. It seems to have the general shape of an exponential distribution, but how can we tell?

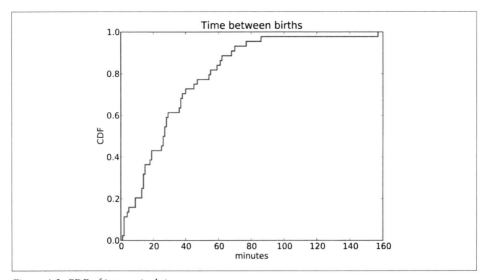

Figure 4-2. CDF of interarrival times

One way is to plot the complementary CDF, $1 - \mathrm{CDF}(x)$, on a log-y scale. For data from an exponential distribution, the result is a straight line. Let's see why that works.

If you plot the complementary CDF (CCDF) of a dataset that you think is exponential, you expect to see a function like:

$$y \approx e^{-\lambda x}$$

Taking the log of both sides yields:

$$\log y \approx -\lambda x$$

So on a log-y scale, the CCDF is a straight line with slope $-\lambda$.

Figure 4-3 shows the CCDF of the interarrivals on a log-y scale. It is not exactly straight, which suggests that the exponential distribution is only an approximation. Most likely the underlying assumption—that a birth is equally likely at any time of day—is not exactly true.

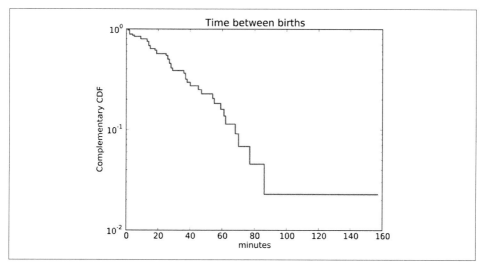

Figure 4-3. CCDF of interarrival times

Exercise 4-1.

For small values of n, we don't expect an empirical distribution to fit a continuous distribution exactly. One way to evaluate the quality of fit is to generate a sample from a continuous distribution and see how well it matches the data.

The function `expovariate` in the `random` module generates random values from an exponential distribution with a given value of λ. Use it to generate 44 values from an exponential distribution with mean 32.6. Plot the CCDF on a log-y scale and compare it to Figure 4-3.

Hint: You can use the function `pyplot.yscale` to plot the y axis on a log scale.

Or, if you use `myplot`, the `Cdf` function takes a boolean option, `complement`, that determines whether to plot the CDF or CCDF, and string options, `xscale` and `yscale`, that transform the axes; to plot a CCDF on a log-y scale:

```
myplot.Cdf(cdf, complement=True, xscale='linear', yscale='log')
```

Exercise 4-2.

Collect the birthdays of the students in your class, sort them, and compute the inter-arrival times in days. Plot the CDF of the interarrival times and the CCDF on a log-y scale. Does it look like an exponential distribution?

The Pareto Distribution

The Pareto distribution is named after the economist Vilfredo Pareto, who used it to describe the distribution of wealth (see *http://wikipedia.org/wiki/Pareto_distribution*). Since then, it has been used to describe phenomena in the natural and social sciences including sizes of cities and towns, sand particles and meteorites, forest fires and earthquakes.

The CDF of the Pareto distribution is:

$$CDF(x) = 1 - \left(\frac{x}{x_m}\right)^{-\alpha}$$

The parameters x_m and α determine the location and shape of the distribution. x_m is the minimum possible value. Figure 4-4 shows the CDF of a Pareto distribution with parameters $x_m = 0.5$ and $\alpha = 1$.

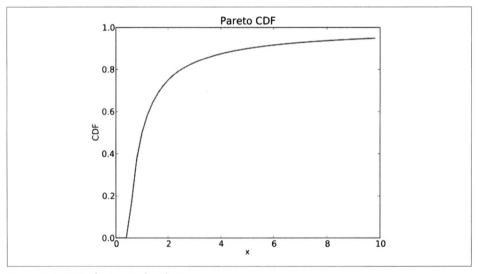

Figure 4-4. CDF of a Pareto distribution

The median of this distribution is:

$$x_m 2^{1/\alpha}$$

which is 1, but the 95th percentile is 10. By contrast, the exponential distribution with median 1 has 95th percentile of only 1.5.

There is a simple visual test that indicates whether an empirical distribution fits a Pareto distribution: on a log-log scale, the CCDF looks like a straight line. If you plot the CCDF of a sample from a Pareto distribution on a linear scale, you expect to see a function like:

$$y \approx \left(\frac{x}{x_m} \right)^{-\alpha}$$

Taking the log of both sides yields:

$$\log y \approx -\alpha (\log x - \log x_m)$$

So if you plot $\log y$ versus $\log x$, it should look like a straight line with slope $-\alpha$ and intercept $\alpha \log x_m$.

Exercise 4-3.

The `random` module provides `paretovariate`, which generates random values from a Pareto distribution. It takes a parameter for α, but not x_m. The default value for x_m is 1; you can generate a distribution with a different parameter by multiplying by x_m.

Write a wrapper function named `paretovariate` that takes α and x_m as parameters and uses `random.paretovariate` to generate values from a two-parameter Pareto distribution.

Use your function to generate a sample from a Pareto distribution. Compute the CCDF and plot it on a log-log scale. Is it a straight line? What is the slope?

Exercise 4-4.

To get a feel for the Pareto distribution, imagine what the world would be like if the distribution of human height were Pareto. Choosing the parameters $x_m = 100$ cm and $\alpha = 1.7$, we get a distribution with a reasonable minimum, 100 cm, and median, 150 cm.

Generate 6 billion random values from this distribution. What is the mean of this sample? What fraction of the population is shorter than the mean? How tall is the tallest person in Pareto World?

Exercise 4-5.

Zipf's law is an observation about how often different words are used. The most common words have very high frequencies, but there are many unusual words, like "hapaxlegomenon," that appear only a few times. Zipf's law predicts that in a body of text, called a "corpus," the distribution of word frequencies is roughly Pareto.

Find a large corpus, in any language, in electronic format. Count how many times each word appears. Find the CCDF of the word counts and plot it on a log-log scale. Does Zipf's law hold? What is the value of α, approximately?

Exercise 4-6.

The Weibull distribution is a generalization of the exponential distribution that comes up in failure analysis (see *http://wikipedia.org/wiki/Weibull_distribution*). Its CDF is:

$$CDF(x) = 1 - e^{-(x/\lambda)^k}$$

Can you find a transformation that makes a Weibull distribution look like a straight line? What do the slope and intercept of the line indicate?

Use `random.weibullvariate` to generate a sample from a Weibull distribution and use it to test your transformation.

The Normal Distribution

The normal distribution, also called Gaussian, is the most commonly used because it describes so many phenomena, at least approximately. It turns out that there is a good reason for its ubiquity, which we will get to in "Central Limit Theorem" on page 68.

The normal distribution has many properties that make it amenable for analysis, but the CDF is not one of them. Unlike the other distributions we have looked at, there is no closed-form expression for the normal CDF; the most common alternative is to write it in terms of the *error function*, which is a special function written erf(x):

$$CDF(x) = \frac{1}{2}\left[1 + \mathrm{erf}\left(\frac{x - \mu}{\sigma\sqrt{2}}\right)\right]$$

$$\mathrm{erf}(x) = \frac{2}{\sqrt{\pi}}\int_0^x e^{-t^2}dt$$

The parameters μ and σ determine the mean and standard deviation of the distribution.

If these formulas make your eyes hurt, don't worry; they are easy to implement in Python.[2] There are many fast and accurate ways to approximate erf(x). You can download one of them from *http://thinkstats.com/erf.py*, which provides functions named `erf` and `NormalCdf`.

Figure 4-5 shows the CDF of the normal distribution with parameters $\mu = 2.0$ and $\sigma = 0.5$. The sigmoid shape of this curve is a recognizable characteristic of a normal distribution.

---

2. As of Python 3.2, it is even easier; `erf` is in the `math` module.

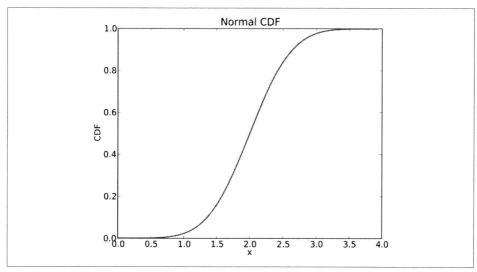

Figure 4-5. CDF of a normal distribution

In the previous chapter, we looked at the distribution of birth weights in the NSFG. Figure 4-6 shows the empirical CDF of weights for all live births and the CDF of a normal distribution with the same mean and variance.

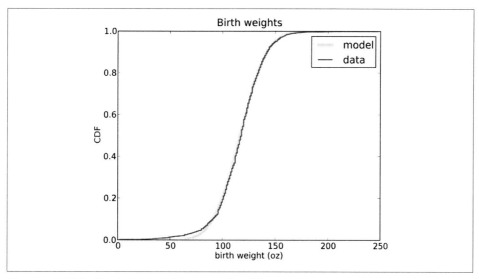

Figure 4-6. CDF of birth weights with a normal model

The normal distribution is a good model for this dataset. A *model* is a useful simplification. In this case it is useful because we can summarize the entire distribution with just two numbers, $\mu = 116.5$ and $\sigma = 19.9$, and the resulting error (difference between the model and the data) is small.

Below the 10th percentile there is a discrepancy between the data and the model; there are more light babies than we would expect in a normal distribution. If we are interested in studying preterm babies, it would be important to get this part of the distribution right, so it might not be appropriate to use the normal model.

Exercise 4-7.

The Wechsler Adult Intelligence Scale is a test that is intended to measure intelligence.[3] Results are transformed so that the distribution of scores in the general population is normal with $\mu = 100$ and $\sigma = 15$.

Use `erf.NormalCdf` to investigate the frequency of rare events in a normal distribution. What fraction of the population has an IQ greater than the mean? What fraction is over 115? 130? 145?

A "six-sigma" event is a value that exceeds the mean by six standard deviations, so a six-sigma IQ is 190. In a world of six billion people, how many do we expect to have an IQ of 190 or more?[4]

Exercise 4-8.

Plot the CDF of pregnancy lengths for all live births. Does it look like a normal distribution?

Compute the mean and variance of the sample and plot the normal distribution with the same parameters. Is the normal distribution a good model for this data? If you had to summarize this distribution with two statistics, what statistics would you choose?

Normal Probability Plot

For the exponential, Pareto, and Weibull distributions, there are simple transformations we can use to test whether a continuous distribution is a good model of a dataset.

For the normal distribution, there is no such transformation, but there is an alternative called a *normal probability plot*. It is based on *rankits*: if you generate *n* values from a normal distribution and sort them, the *k*th rankit is the mean of the distribution for the *k*th value.

---

3. Whether it does or not is a fascinating controversy that I invite you to investigate at your leisure.

4. On this topic, you might be interested to read *http://wikipedia.org/wiki/Christopher_Langan*.

Exercise 4-9.

Write a function called `Sample` that generates six samples from a normal distribution with $\mu = 0$ and $\sigma = 1$. Sort and return the values.

Write a function called `Samples` that calls `Sample` 1,000 times and returns a list of 1,000 lists.

If you apply `zip` to this list of lists, the result is six lists with 1,000 values in each. Compute the mean of each of these lists and print the results. I predict that you will get something like this:

{–1.2672, –0.6418, –0.2016, 0.2016, 0.6418, 1.2672}

If you increase the number of times you call `Sample`, the results should converge on these values.

Computing rankits exactly is moderately difficult, but there are numerical methods for approximating them. And there is a quick-and-dirty method that is even easier to implement:

1. From a normal distribution with $\mu = 0$ and $\sigma = 1$, generate a sample with the same size as your dataset and sort it.
2. Sort the values in the dataset.
3. Plot the sorted values from your dataset versus the random values.

For large datasets, this method works well. For smaller datasets, you can improve it by generating $m(n+1) - 1$ values from a normal distribution, where n is the size of the dataset and m is a multiplier. Then select every mth element, starting with the mth.

This method works with other distributions as well, as long as you know how to generate a random sample.

Figure 4-7 is a quick-and-dirty normal probability plot for the birth weight data.

The curvature in this plot suggests that there are deviations from a normal distribution; nevertheless, it is a good (enough) model for many purposes.

Exercise 4-10.

Write a function called `NormalPlot` that takes a sequence of values and generates a normal probability plot. You can download a solution from *http://thinkstats.com/rankit .py*.

Use the running speeds from `relay.py` to generate a normal probability plot. Is the normal distribution a good model for this data? You can download a solution from *http://thinkstats.com/relay_normal.py*.

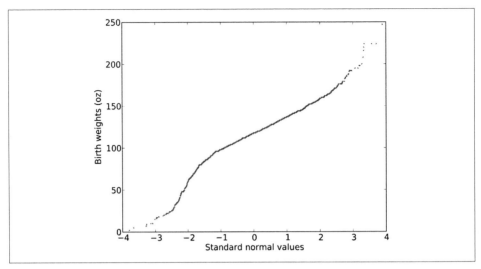

Figure 4-7. Normal probability plot of birth weights

The Lognormal Distribution

If the logarithms of a set of values have a normal distribution, the values have a *log-normal* distribution. The CDF of the lognormal distribution is the same as the CDF of the normal distribution, with log x substituted for x.

$$CDF_{lognormal}(x) = CDF_{normal}(\log x)$$

The parameters of the lognormal distribution are usually denoted μ and σ. But remember that these parameters are *not* the mean and standard deviation; the mean of a lognormal distribution is $\exp(\mu + \sigma^2/2)$ and the standard deviation is ugly.[5]

It turns out that the distribution of weights for adults is approximately lognormal.[6]

The National Center for Chronic Disease Prevention and Health Promotion conducts an annual survey as part of the Behavioral Risk Factor Surveillance System (BRFSS).[7] In 2008, they interviewed 414,509 respondents and asked about their demographics, health, and health risks.

5. See *http://wikipedia.org/wiki/Log-normal_distribution*.

6. I was tipped off to this possibility by a comment (without citation) at *http://mathworld.wolfram.com/LogNormalDistribution.html*. Subsequently I found a paper that proposes the log transform and suggests a cause: Penman and Johnson, "The Changing Shape of the Body Mass Index Distribution Curve in the Population," Preventing Chronic Disease, 2006 July; 3(3): A74. Online at *http://www.ncbi.nlm.nih.gov/pmc/articles/PMC1636707*.

7. Centers for Disease Control and Prevention (CDC). Behavioral Risk Factor Surveillance System Survey Data. Atlanta, Georgia: U.S. Department of Health and Human Services, Centers for Disease Control and Prevention, 2008.

Among the data they collected are the weights in kilograms of 398,484 respondents. Figure 4-8 shows the distribution of log w, where w is weight in kilograms, along with a normal model.

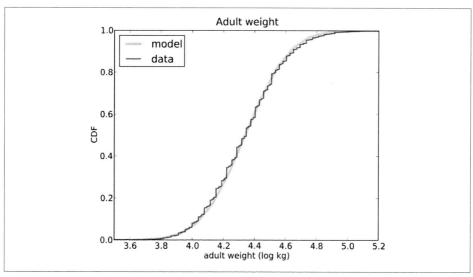

Figure 4-8. CDF of adult weights (log transform)

The normal model is a good fit for the data, although the highest weights exceed what we expect from the normal model even after the log transform. Since the distribution of log w fits a normal distribution, we conclude that w fits a lognormal distribution.

Exercise 4-11.

Download the BRFSS data from *http://thinkstats.com/CDBRFS08.ASC.gz*, and my code for reading it from *http://thinkstats.com/brfss.py*. Run `brfss.py` and confirm that it prints summary statistics for a few of the variables.

Write a program that reads adult weights from the BRFSS and generates normal probability plots for w and log w. You can download a solution from *http://thinkstats.com/brfss_figs.py*.

Exercise 4-12.

The distribution of populations for cities and towns has been proposed as an example of a real-world phenomenon that can be described with a Pareto distribution.

The U.S. Census Bureau publishes data on the population of every incorporated city and town in the United States. I have written a small program that downloads this data and stores it in a file. You can download it from *http://thinkstats.com/populations.py*.

1. Read over the program to make sure you know what it does; then run it to download and process the data.

2. Write a program that computes and plots the distribution of populations for the 14,593 cities and towns in the dataset.

3. Plot the CDF on linear and log-x scales so you can get a sense of the shape of the distribution. Then plot the CCDF on a log-log scale to see if it has the characteristic shape of a Pareto distribution.

4. Try out the other transformations and plots in this chapter to see if there is a better model for this data.

What conclusion do you draw about the distribution of sizes for cities and towns? You can download a solution from *http://thinkstats.com/populations_cdf.py*.

Exercise 4-13.

The Internal Revenue Service of the United States (IRS) provides data about income taxes at *http://irs.gov/taxstats*.

One of their files, containing information about individual incomes for 2008, is available from *http://thinkstats.com/08in11si.csv*. I converted it to a text format called CSV, which stands for "comma-separated values"; you can read it using the csv module.

Extract the distribution of incomes from this dataset. Are any of the continuous distributions in this chapter a good model of the data? You can download a solution from *http://thinkstats.com/irs.py*.

Why Model?

At the beginning of this chapter, I said that many real-world phenomena can be modeled with continuous distributions. "So what?", you might ask.

Like all models, continuous distributions are abstractions, which means they leave out details that are considered irrelevant. For example, an observed distribution might have measurement errors or quirks that are specific to the sample; continuous models smooth out these idiosyncrasies.

Continuous models are also a form of data compression. When a model fits a dataset well, a small set of parameters can summarize a large amount of data.

It is sometimes surprising when data from a natural phenomenon fit a continuous distribution, but these observations can lead to insight into physical systems. Sometimes we can explain why an observed distribution has a particular form. For example, Pareto distributions are often the result of generative processes with positive feedback (so-called preferential attachment processes: see *http://wikipedia.org/wiki/Preferential _attachment.*).

Continuous distributions lend themselves to mathematical analysis, as we will see in Chapter 6.

Generating Random Numbers

Continuous CDFs are also useful for generating random numbers. If there is an efficient way to compute the inverse CDF, ICDF(p), we can generate random values with the appropriate distribution by choosing from a uniform distribution from 0 to 1, then choosing:

x = ICDF(p)

For example, the CDF of the exponential distribution is:

$p = 1 - e^{-\lambda x}$

Solving for x yields:

$x = -\log (1 - p) / \lambda$

So in Python we can write:

```
def expovariate(lam):
    p = random.random()
    x = -math.log(1-p) / lam
    return x
```

I called the parameter `lam` because `lambda` is a Python keyword. Most implementations of `random.random` can return 0 but not 1, so $1 - p$ can be 1 but not 0, which is good, because log 0 is undefined.

Exercise 4-14.

Write a function named `weibullvariate` that takes `lam` and `k` and returns a random value from the Weibull distribution with those parameters.

Glossary

continuous distribution
> A distribution described by a continuous function.

corpus
> A body of text used as a sample of a language.

empirical distribution
> The distribution of values in a sample.

error function
> A special mathematical function, so named because it comes up in the study of measurement errors.

hapaxlegomenon
   A word that appears only once in a corpus. It appears twice in this book, so far.

interarrival time
   The elapsed time between two events.

model
   A useful simplification. Continuous distributions are often good models of more complex empirical distributions.

normal probability plot
   A plot of the sorted values in a sample versus the expected value for each if their distribution is normal.

rankit
   The expected value of an element in a sorted list of values from a normal distribution.

CHAPTER 5

Probability

In Chapter 2, I said that a probability is a frequency expressed as a fraction of the sample size. That's one definition of probability, but it's not the only one. In fact, the meaning of probability is a topic of some controversy.

We'll start with the uncontroversial parts and work our way up. There is general agreement that a probability is a real value between 0 and 1 that is intended to be a quantitative measure corresponding to the qualitative notion that some things are more likely than others.

The "things" we assign probabilities to are called *events*. If E represents an event, then $P(E)$ represents the probability that E will occur. A situation where E might or might not happen is called a *trial*.

As an example, suppose you have a standard six-sided die and want to know the probability of rolling a six. Each roll is a trial. Each time a six appears is considered a *success*; other trials are considered *failures*. These terms are used even in scenarios where "success" is bad and "failure" is good.

If we have a finite sample of n trials and we observe s successes, the probability of success is s/n. If the set of trials is infinite, defining probabilities is a little trickier, but most people are willing to accept probabilistic claims about a hypothetical series of identical trials, like tossing a coin or rolling a die.

We start to run into trouble when we talk about probabilities of unique events. For example, we might like to know the probability that a candidate will win an election. But every election is unique, so there is no series of identical trials to consider.

In cases like this, some people would say that the notion of probability does not apply. This position is sometimes called *frequentism* because it defines probability in terms of frequencies. If there is no set of identical trials, there is no probability.

Frequentism is philosophically safe, but frustrating because it limits the scope of probability to physical systems that are either random (like atomic decay) or so unpredictable that we model them as random (like a tumbling die). Anything involving people is pretty much off the table.

An alternative is *Bayesianism*, which defines probability as a degree of belief that an event will occur. By this definition, the notion of probability can be applied in almost any circumstance. One difficulty with Bayesian probability is that it depends on a person's state of knowledge; people with different information might have different degrees of belief about the same event. For this reason, many people think that Bayesian probabilities are more subjective than frequency probabilities.

As an example, what is the probability that Thaksin Shinawatra is the Prime Minister of Thailand? A frequentist would say that there is no probability for this event because there is no set of trials. Thaksin either is, or is not, the PM; it's not a question of probability.

In contrast, a Bayesian would be willing to assign a probability to this event based on his or her state of knowledge. For example, if you remember that there was a coup in Thailand in 2006, and you are pretty sure Thaksin was the PM who was ousted, you might assign a probability like 0.1, which acknowledges the possibility that your recollection is incorrect, or that Thaksin has been reinstated.

If you consult Wikipedia, you will learn that Thaksin is not the PM of Thailand (at the time I am writing). Based on this information, you might revise your probability estimate to 0.01, reflecting the possibility that Wikipedia is wrong.

Rules of Probability

For frequency probabilities, we can derive rules that relate probabilities of different events. Probably the best known of these rules is:

$P(A \text{ and } B) = P(A) P(B)$ Warning: not always true!

where $P(A \text{ and } B)$ is the probability that events A and B both occur. This formula is easy to remember; the only problem is that it is *not always true*. This formula only applies if A and B are *independent*, which means that if I know A occurred, that doesn't change the probability of B, and vice versa.

For example, if A is tossing a coin and getting heads, and B is rolling a die and getting 1, A and B are independent, because the coin toss doesn't tell me anything about the die roll.

But if I roll two dice, and A is getting at least one six, and B is getting two sixes, A and B are not independent, because if I know that A occurred, the probability of B is higher, and if I know B occurred, the probability of A is 1.

When A and B are not independent, it is often useful to compute the conditional probability, $P(A|B)$, which is the probability of A given that we know B occurred:

$$P(A|B) = \frac{P(A \text{ and } B)}{P(B)}$$

From that, we can derive the general relation

$P(A \text{ and } B) = P(A) \, P(B|A)$

This might not be as easy to remember, but if you translate it into English, it should make sense: "The chance of both things happening is the chance that the first one happens, and then the second one given the first."

There is nothing special about the order of events, so we could also write

$P(A \text{ and } B) = P(B) \, P(A|B)$

These relationships hold whether A and B are independent or not. If they are independent, then $P(A|B) = P(A)$, which gets us back where we started.

Because all probabilities are in the range 0 to 1, it is easy to show that

$P(A \text{ and } B) \leq P(A)$

To picture this, imagine a club that only admits people who satisfy some requirement, A. Now suppose they add a new requirement for membership, B. It seems obvious that the club will get smaller, or stay the same if it happens that all the members satisfy B. But there are some scenarios where people are surprisingly bad at this kind of analysis. For examples and discussion of this phenomenon, see *http://wikipedia.org/wiki/Con junction_fallacy*.

Exercise 5-1.

If I roll two dice and the total is eight, what is the chance that one of the dice is a six?

Exercise 5-2.

If I roll 100 dice, what is the chance of getting all sixes? What is the chance of getting no sixes?

Exercise 5-3.

The following questions are adapted from Mlodinow, *The Drunkard's Walk*.

1. If a family has two children, what is the chance that they have two girls?
2. If a family has two children and we know that at least one of them is a girl, what is the chance that they have two girls?
3. If a family has two children and we know that the older one is a girl, what is the chance that they have two girls?
4. If a family has two children and we know that at least one of them is a girl named Florida, what is the chance that they have two girls?

You can assume that the probability that any child is a girl is 1/2, and that the children in a family are independent trials (in more ways than one). You can also assume that the percentage of girls named Florida is small.

Monty Hall

The Monty Hall problem might be the most contentious question in the history of probability. The scenario is simple, but the correct answer is so counterintuitive that many people just can't accept it, and many smart people have embarrassed themselves not just by getting it wrong but by arguing the wrong side, aggressively, in public.

Monty Hall was the original host of the game show *Let's Make a Deal*. The Monty Hall problem is based on one of the regular games on the show. If you are on the show, here's what happens:

- Monty shows you three closed doors and tells you that there is a prize behind each door: one prize is a car, the other two are less valuable prizes like peanut butter and fake fingernails. The prizes are arranged at random.
- The object of the game is to guess which door has the car. If you guess right, you get to keep the car.
- So you pick a door, which we will call Door A. We'll call the other doors B and C.
- Before opening the door you chose, Monty likes to increase the suspense by opening either Door B or C, whichever does not have the car. (If the car is actually behind Door A, Monty can safely open B or C, so he chooses one at random).
- Then Monty offers you the option to stick with your original choice or switch to the one remaining unopened door.

The question is, should you "stick" or "switch" or does it make no difference?

Most people have the strong intuition that it makes no difference. There are two doors left, they reason, so the chance that the car is behind Door A is 50%.

But that is wrong. In fact, the chance of winning if you stick with Door A is only 1/3; if you switch, your chances are 2/3. I will explain why, but I don't expect you to believe me.

The key is to realize that there are three possible scenarios: the car is behind Door A, B, or C. Since the prizes are arranged at random, the probability of each scenario is 1/3.

If your strategy is to stick with Door A, then you will win only in Scenario A, which has probability 1/3.

If your strategy is to switch, you will win in either Scenario B or Scenario C, so the total probability of winning is 2/3.

If you are not completely convinced by this argument, you are in good company. When a friend presented this solution to Paul Erdős, he replied, "No, that is impossible. It should make no difference."[1]

---

1. See Hoffman, *The Man Who Loved Only Numbers*, page 83.

No amount of argument could convince him. In the end, it took a computer simulation to bring him around.

Exercise 5-4.

Write a program that simulates the Monty Hall problem and use it to estimate the probability of winning if you stick and if you switch.

Then read the discussion of the problem at *http://wikipedia.org/wiki/Monty_Hall_problem*.

Which do you find more convincing, the simulation or the arguments, and why?

Exercise 5-5.

To understand the Monty Hall problem, it is important to realize that by deciding which door to open, Monty is giving you information. To see why this matters, imagine the case where Monty doesn't know where the prizes are, so he chooses Door B or C at random.

If he opens the door with the car, the game is over, you lose, and you don't get to choose whether to switch or stick.

Otherwise, are you better off switching or sticking?

Poincaré

Henri Poincaré was a French mathematician who taught at the Sorbonne around 1900. The following anecdote about him is probably fabricated, but it makes an interesting probability problem.

Supposedly, Poincaré suspected that his local bakery was selling loaves of bread that were lighter than the advertised weight of 1 kg, so every day for a year he bought a loaf of bread, brought it home and weighed it. At the end of the year, he plotted the distribution of his measurements and showed that it fit a normal distribution with mean 950 g and standard deviation 50 g. He brought this evidence to the bread police, who gave the baker a warning.

For the next year, Poincaré continued the practice of weighing his bread every day. At the end of the year, he found that the average weight was 1,000 g, just as it should be, but again he complained to the bread police, and this time they fined the baker.

Why? Because the shape of the distribution was asymmetric. Unlike the normal distribution, it was skewed to the right, which is consistent with the hypothesis that the baker was still making 950 g loaves, but deliberately giving Poincaré the heavier ones.

Exercise 5-6.

Write a program that simulates a baker who chooses n loaves from a distribution with mean 950 g and standard deviation 50 g, and gives the heaviest one to Poincaré. What value of n yields a distribution with mean 1000 g? What is the standard deviation?

Compare this distribution to a normal distribution with the same mean and the same standard deviation. Is the difference in the shape of the distribution big enough to convince the bread police?

Exercise 5-7.

If you go to a dance where partners are paired up randomly, what percentage of opposite sex couples will you see where the woman is taller than the man?

In the BRFSS (see "The Lognormal Distribution" on page 42), the distribution of heights is roughly normal, with parameters $\mu = 178$ cm and $\sigma^2 = 59.4$ cm for men, and $\mu = 163$ cm and $\sigma^2 = 52.8$ cm for women.

As an aside, you might notice that the standard deviation for men is higher and wonder whether men's heights are more variable. To compare variability between groups, it is useful to compute the *coefficient of variation*, which is the standard deviation as a fraction of the mean, σ/μ. By this measure, women's heights are slightly more variable.

Another Rule of Probability

If two events are *mutually exclusive*, that means that only one of them can happen, so the conditional probabilities are 0:

$P(A|B) = P(B|A) = 0$

In this case, it is easy to compute the probability of either event:

$P(A \text{ or } B) = P(A) + P(B)$ Warning: not always true.

But remember that this only applies if the events are mutually exclusive. In general, the probability of A or B or both is:

$P(A \text{ or } B) = P(A) + P(B) - P(A \text{ and } B)$

The reason we have to subtract off $P(A \text{ and } B)$ is that otherwise it gets counted twice. For example, if I flip two coins, the chance of getting at least one tails is $1/2 + 1/2 - 1/4$. I have to subtract 1/4 because otherwise I am counting heads-heads twice. The problem becomes even clearer if I toss three coins.

Exercise 5-8.

If I roll two dice, what is the chance of rolling at least one six?

Exercise 5-9.

What is the general formula for the probability of A or B but not both?

Binomial Distribution

If I roll 100 dice, the chance of getting all sixes is $(1/6)^{100}$. And the chance of getting no sixes is $(5/6)^{100}$.

Those cases are easy, but more generally, we might like to know the chance of getting k sixes, for all values of k from 0 to 100. The answer is the *binomial distribution*, which has this PMF:

$$\text{PMF}(k) = \binom{n}{k} p^k (1-p)^{n-k}$$

where n is the number of trials, p is the probability of success, and k is the number of successes.

The *binomial coefficient* is pronounced "n choose k", and it can be computed directly like this:

$$\binom{n}{k} = \frac{n!}{k!(n-k)!}$$

Or recursively like this

$$\binom{n}{k} = \binom{n-1}{k} + \binom{n-1}{k-1}$$

with two base cases: if $n = 0$ the result is 0; if $k = 0$ the result is 1. If you download *http://thinkstats.com/thinkstats.py* you will see a function named `Binom` that computes the binomial coefficient with reasonable efficiency.

Exercise 5-10.

If you flip a coin 100 times, you expect about 50 heads, but what is the probability of getting exactly 50 heads?

Streaks and Hot Spots

People do not have very good intuition for random processes. If you ask people to generate "random" numbers, they tend to generate sequences that are random-looking, but actually more ordered than real random sequences. Conversely, if you show them a real random sequence, they tend to see patterns where there are none.

An example of the second phenomenon is that many people believe in "streaks" in sports: a player that has been successful recently is said to have a "hot hand"; a player that has been unsuccessful is "in a slump."

Statisticians have tested these hypotheses in a number of sports, and the consistent result is that there is no such thing as a streak.[2] If you assume that each attempt is independent of previous attempts, you will see occasional long strings of successes or failures. These apparent streaks are not sufficient evidence that there is any relationship between successive attempts.

A related phenomenon is the clustering illusion, which is the tendency to see clusters in spatial patterns that are actually random (see *http://wikipedia.org/wiki/Clustering_illusion*).

To test whether an apparent cluster is likely to be meaningful, we can simulate the behavior of a random system to see whether it is likely to produce a similar cluster. This process is called *Monte Carlo* simulation because generating random numbers is reminiscent of casino games (and Monte Carlo is famous for its casino).

Exercise 5-11.

If there are 10 players in a basketball game and each one takes 15 shots during the course of the game, and each shot has a 50% probability of going in, what is the probability that you will see, in a given game, at least one player who hits 10 shots in a row? If you watch a season of 82 games, what are the chances you will see at least one streak of 10 hits or misses?

This problem demonstrates some strengths and weaknesses of Monte Carlo simulation. A strength is that it is often easy and fast to write a simulation, and no great knowledge of probability is required. A weakness is that estimating the probability of rare events can take a long time! A little bit of analysis can save a lot of computing.

Exercise 5-12.

In 1941, Joe DiMaggio got at least one hit in 56 consecutive games.[3] Many baseball fans consider this streak the greatest achievement in any sport in history, because it was so unlikely.

Use a Monte Carlo simulation to estimate the probability that any player in major league baseball will have a hitting streak of 57 or more games in the next century.

2. For example, see Gilovich, Vallone, and Tversky, "The hot hand in basketball: On the misperception of random sequences," 1985.

3. See *http://wikipedia.org/wiki/Hitting_streak*.

Exercise 5-13.

A cancer cluster is defined by the Centers for Disease Control (CDC) as "greater-than-expected number of cancer cases that occurs within a group of people in a geographic area over a period of time."[4]

Many people interpret a cancer cluster as evidence of an environmental hazard, but many scientists and statisticians think that investigating cancer clusters is a waste of time.[5] Why? One reason (among several) is that identifying cancer clusters is a classic case of the Sharpshooter Fallacy (see *http://wikipedia.org/wiki/Texas_sharpshooter_fallacy*).

Nevertheless, when someone reports a cancer cluster, the CDC is obligated to investigate. According to their web page:

> Investigators develop a "case" definition, a time period of concern, and the population at risk. They then calculate the expected number of cases and compare them to the observed number. A cluster is confirmed when the observed/expected ratio is greater than 1.0, and the difference is statistically significant.

1. Suppose that a particular cancer has an incidence of one case per thousand people per year. If you follow a particular cohort of 100 people for 10 years, you would expect to see about one case. If you saw two cases, that would not be very surprising, but more than than two would be rare.

   Write a program that simulates a large number of cohorts over a 10-year period and estimates the distribution of total cases.

2. An observation is considered statistically significant if its probability by chance alone, called a p-value, is less than 5%. In a cohort of 100 people over 10 years, how many cases would you have to see to meet this criterion?

3. Now imagine that you divide a population of 10,000 people into 100 cohorts and follow them for 10 years. What is the chance that at least one of the cohorts will have a "statistically significant" cluster? What if we require a p-value of 1%?

4. Now imagine that you arrange 10,000 people in a 100 × 100 grid and follow them for 10 years. What is the chance that there will be at least one 10 × 10 block anywhere in the grid with a statistically significant cluster?

5. Finally, imagine that you follow a grid of 10,000 people for 30 years. What is the chance that there will be a 10-year interval at some point with a 10 × 10 block anywhere in the grid with a statistically significant cluster?

---

4. From *http://cdc.gov/nceh/clusters/about.htm*.

5. See Gawande, "The Cancer Cluster Myth," *New Yorker*, Feb 8, 1997.

Bayes's Theorem

Bayes's theorem is a relationship between the conditional probabilities of two events. A conditional probability, often written $P(A|B)$ is the probability that Event A will occur given that we know that Event B has occurred. Bayes's theorem states:

$$P(A|B) = \frac{P(B|A)P(A)}{P(B)}$$

To see that this is true, it helps to write $P(A \text{ and } B)$, which is the probability that A and B occur

$$P(A \text{ and } B) = P(A)\ P(B|A)$$

But it is also true that

$$P(A \text{ and } B) = P(B)\ P(A|B)$$

So

$$P(B)\ P(A|B) = P(A)\ P(B|A)$$

Dividing through by $P(B)$ yields Bayes's theorem.[6]

Bayes's theorem is often interpreted as a statement about how a body of evidence, E, affects the probability of a hypothesis, H:

$$P(H|E) = P(H)\frac{P(E|H)}{P(E)}$$

In words, this equation says that the probability of H after you have seen E is the product of $P(H)$, which is the probability of H before you saw the evidence, and the ratio of $P(E|H)$, the probability of seeing the evidence assuming that H is true, and $P(E)$, the probability of seeing the evidence under any circumstances (H true or not).

This way of reading Bayes's theorem is called the "diachronic" interpretation because it describes how the probability of a hypothesis gets *updated* over time, usually in light of new evidence. In this context, $P(H)$ is called the *prior* probability and $P(H|E)$ is called the *posterior*. $P(E|H)$ is the *likelihood of the evidence*, and $P(E)$ is the *normalizing constant*.

A classic use of Bayes's theorem is the interpretation of clinical tests. For example, routine testing for illegal drug use is increasingly common in workplaces and schools (see *http://aclu.org/drugpolicy/testing*). The companies that perform these tests maintain that the tests are sensitive, which means that they are likely to produce a positive result if there are drugs (or metabolites) in a sample, and specific, which means that they are likely to yield a negative result if there are no drugs.

---

6. See *http://wikipedia.org/wiki/Q.E.D.!*

Studies from the Journal of the American Medical Association[7] estimate that the sensitivity of common drug tests is about 60% and the specificity is about 99%.

Now suppose these tests are applied to a workforce where the actual rate of drug use is 5%. Of the employees who test positive, how many of them actually use drugs?

In Bayesian terms, we want to compute the probability of drug use given a positive test, $P(D|E)$. By Bayes's theorem:

$$P(D|E) = P(D)\frac{P(E|D)}{P(E)}$$

The prior, $P(D)$ is the probability of drug use before we see the outcome of the test, which is 5%. The likelihood, $P(E|D)$, is the probability of a positive test assuming drug use, which is the sensitivity.

The normalizing constant, $P(E)$ is a little harder to evaluate. We have to consider two possibilities, $P(E|D)$ and $P(E|N)$, where N is the hypothesis that the subject of the test does not use drugs:

$P(E) = P(D) \, P(E|D) + P(N) \, P(E|N)$

The probability of a false positive, $P(E|N)$, is the complement of the specificity, or 1%.

Putting it together, we have

$$P(D|E) = \frac{P(D)P(E|D)}{P(D)P(E|D) + P(N)P(E|N)}$$

Plugging in the given values yields $P(D|E) = 0.76$, which means that of the people who test positive, about 1 in 4 is innocent.

Exercise 5-14.

Write a program that takes the actual rate of drug use, and the sensitivity and specificity of the test, and uses Bayes's theorem to compute $P(D|E)$.

Suppose the same test is applied to a population where the actual rate of drug use is 1%. What is the probability that someone who tests positive is actually a drug user?

Exercise 5-15.

This exercise is from *http://wikipedia.org/wiki/Bayesian_inference*.

> Suppose there are two full bowls of cookies. Bowl 1 has 10 chocolate chip and 30 plain cookies, while Bowl 2 has 20 of each. Our friend Fred picks a bowl at random, and then picks a cookie at random. The cookie turns out to be a plain one. How probable is it that Fred picked it out of Bowl 1?

---

7. I got these numbers from Gleason and Barnum, "Predictive Probabilities In Employee Drug-Testing," at *http://piercelaw.edu/risk/vol2/winter/gleason.htm*.

Exercise 5-16.

The blue M&M was introduced in 1995. Before then, the color mix in a bag of plain M&Ms was (30% Brown, 20% Yellow, 20% Red, 10% Green, 10% Orange, 10% Tan). Afterward it was (24% Blue , 20% Green, 16% Orange, 14% Yellow, 13% Red, 13% Brown).

A friend of mine has two bags of M&Ms, and he tells me that one is from 1994 and one from 1996. He won't tell me which is which, but he gives me one M&M from each bag. One is yellow and one is green. What is the probability that the yellow M&M came from the 1994 bag?

Exercise 5-17.

This exercise is adapted from MacKay, *Information Theory, Inference, and Learning Algorithms*:

Elvis Presley had a twin brother who died at birth. According to the Wikipedia article on twins:

> Twins are estimated to be approximately 1.9% of the world population, with monozygotic twins making up 0.2% of the total—and 8% of all twins.

What is the probability that Elvis was an identical twin?

Glossary

Bayesianism
> A more general interpretation that uses probability to represent a subjective degree of belief.

coefficient of variation
> A statistic that measures spread, normalized by central tendency, for comparison between distributions with different means.

event
> Something that may or may not occur, with some probability.

failure
> A trail in which no event occurs.

frequentism
> A strict interpretation of probability that only applies to a series of identical trials.

independent
> Two events are independent if the occurrence of one has no effect on the probability of another.

likelihood of the evidence
> One of the terms in Bayes's theorem, the probability of the evidence conditioned on a hypothesis.

Monte Carlo simulation

A method of computing probabilities by simulating random processes (see *http://wikipedia.org/wiki/Monte_Carlo_method*).

normalizing constant

The denominator of Bayes's Theorem, used to normalize the result to be a probability.

posterior

A probability computed by a Bayesian update.

prior

A probability before a Bayesian update.

success

A trial in which an event occurs.

trial

One in a series of occasions when an event might occur.

update

The process of using data to revise a probability.

CHAPTER 6

Operations on Distributions

Skewness

Skewness is a statistic that measures the asymmetry of a distribution. Given a sequence of values, x_i, the sample skewness is:

$$g_1 = m_3/m_2^{3/2}$$

$$m_2 = \frac{1}{n}\sum_i (x_i - \mu)^2$$

$$m_3 = \frac{1}{n}\sum_i (x_i - \mu)^3$$

You might recognize m_2 as the mean squared deviation (also known as variance); m_3 is the mean cubed deviation.

Negative skewness indicates that a distribution "skews left"; that is, it extends farther to the left than the right. Positive skewness indicates that a distribution skews right.

In practice, computing the skewness of a sample is usually not a good idea. If there are any outliers, they have a disproportionate effect on g_1.

Another way to evaluate the asymmetry of a distribution is to look at the relationship between the mean and median. Extreme values have more effect on the mean than the median, so in a distribution that skews left, the mean is less than the median.

Pearson's median skewness coefficient is an alternative measure of skewness that ex-plicitly captures the relationship between the mean, μ, and the median, $\mu_{1/2}$:

$$g_p = 3(\mu - \mu_{1/2})/\sigma$$

This statistic is *robust*, which means that it is less vulnerable to the effect of outliers.

Exercise 6-1.

Write a function named `Skewness` that computes g_1 for a sample.

Compute the skewness for the distributions of pregnancy length and birth weight. Are the results consistent with the shape of the distributions?

Write a function named `PearsonSkewness` that computes g_p for these distributions. How does g_p compare to g_1?

Exercise 6-2.

The "Lake Wobegon effect" is an amusing nickname[1] for *illusory superiority*, which is the tendency for people to overestimate their abilities relative to others. For example, in some surveys, more than 80% of respondents believe that they are better than the average driver (see *http://wikipedia.org/wiki/Illusory_superiority*).

If we interpret "average" to mean median, then this result is logically impossible, but if "average" is the mean, this result is possible, although unlikely.

What percentage of the population has more than the average number of legs?

Exercise 6-3.

The Internal Revenue Service of the United States (IRS) provides data about income taxes, and other statistics, at *http://irs.gov/taxstats*. If you did Exercise 4-13, you have already worked with this data; otherwise, follow the instructions there to extract the distribution of incomes from this dataset.

What fraction of the population reports a taxable income below the mean?

Compute the median, mean, skewness, and Pearson's skewness of the income data. Because the data has been binned, you will have to make some approximations.

The Gini coefficient is a measure of income inequality. Read about it at *http://wikipedia .org/wiki/Gini_coefficient* and write a function called `Gini` that computes it for the income distribution.

Hint: use the PMF to compute the relative mean difference (see *http://wikipedia.org/ wiki/Mean_difference*).

You can download a solution to this exercise from *http://thinkstats.com/gini.py*.

Random Variables

A *random variable* represents a process that generates a random number. Random variables are usually written with a capital letter, like X. When you see a random variable, you should think "a value selected from a distribution."

For example, the formal definition of the cumulative distribution function is:

---

1. If you don't get it, see *http://wikipedia.org/wiki/Lake_Wobegon*.

$$\text{CDF}_X(x) = P(X \le x)$$

I have avoided this notation until now because it is so awful, but here's what it means: the CDF of the random variable X, evaluated for a particular value x, is defined as the probability that a value generated by the random process X is less than or equal to x.

As a computer scientist, I find it helpful to think of a random variable as an object that provides a method, which I will call generate, that uses a random process to generate values.

For example, here is a definition for a class that represents random variables:

```
class RandomVariable(object):
    """Parent class for all random variables."""
```

And here is a random variable with an exponential distribution:

```
class Exponential(RandomVariable):
    def __init__(self, lam):
        self.lam = lam

    def generate(self):
        return random.expovariate(self.lam)
```

The init method takes the parameter, λ, and stores it as an attribute. The generate method returns a random value from the exponential distribution with that parameter.

Each time you invoke generate, you get a different value. The value you get is called a *random variate*, which is why many function names in the random module include the word "variate."

If I were just generating exponential variates, I would not bother to define a new class; I would use random.expovariate. But for other distributions, it might be useful to use RandomVariable objects. For example, the Erlang distribution is a continuous distribution with parameters λ and k (see *http://wikipedia.org/wiki/Erlang_distribution*).

One way to generate values from an Erlang distribution is to add k values from an exponential distribution with the same λ. Here's an implementation:

```
class Erlang(RandomVariable):
    def __init__(self, lam, k):
        self.lam = lam
        self.k = k
        self.expo = Exponential(lam)

    def generate(self):
        total = 0
        for i in range(self.k):
            total += self.expo.generate()
        return total
```

The init method creates an Exponential object with the given parameter; then generate uses it. In general, the init method can take any set of parameters and the generate function can implement any random process.

Exercise 6-4.

Write a definition for a class that represents a random variable with a Gumbel distribution (see *http://wikipedia.org/wiki/Gumbel_distribution*).

PDFs

The derivative of a CDF is called a *probability density function*, or *PDF*. For example, the PDF of an exponential distribution is

$$\text{PDF}_{expo}(x) = \lambda e^{-\lambda x}$$

The PDF of a normal distribution is

$$\text{PDF}_{normal}(x) = \frac{1}{\sigma \sqrt{2\pi}} \exp \left[-\frac{1}{2} \left(\frac{x - \mu}{\sigma} \right)^2 \right]$$

Evaluating a PDF for a particular value of x is usually not useful. The result is not a probability; it is a probability *density*.

In physics, density is mass per unit of volume; in order to get a mass, you have to multiply by volume or, if the density is not constant, you have to integrate over volume.

Similarly, probability density measures probability per unit of x. In order to get a probability mass,[2] you have to integrate over x. For example, if x is a random variable whose PDF is PDF_X, we can compute the probability that a value from X falls between –0.5 and 0.5:

$$P(-0.5 \le X < 0.5) = \int_{-0.5}^{0.5} \text{PDF}_X(x)dx$$

Or, since the CDF is the integral of the PDF, we can write

$$P(-0.5 \le X < 0.5) = \text{CDF}_X(0.5) - \text{CDF}_X(-0.5)$$

For some distributions, we can evaluate the CDF explicitly, so we would use the second option. Otherwise, we usually have to integrate the PDF numerically.

---

2. To take the analogy one step farther, the mean of a distribution is its center of mass, and the variance is its moment of inertia.

Exercise 6-5.

What is the probability that a value chosen from an exponential distribution with parameter λ falls between 1 and 20? Express your answer as a function of λ. Keep this result handy; we will use it in "Censored Data" on page 92.

Exercise 6-6.

In the BRFSS (see "The Lognormal Distribution" on page 42), the distribution of heights is roughly normal, with parameters $\mu = 178$ cm and $\sigma^2 = 59.4$ cm for men, and $\mu = 163$ cm and $\sigma^2 = 52.8$ cm for women.

In order to join Blue Man Group, you have to be male between 5'10" and 6'1" (see *http://bluemancasting.com*). What percentage of the U.S. male population is in this range? Hint: see "The Normal Distribution" on page 38.

Convolution

Suppose we have two random variables, X and Y, with distributions CDF_X and CDF_Y. What is the distribution of the sum $Z = X + Y$?

One option is to write a RandomVariable object that generates the sum:

```
class Sum(RandomVariable):
    def __init__(X, Y):
        self.X = X
        self.Y = Y

    def generate():
        return X.generate() + Y.generate()
```

Given any RandomVariables, X and Y, we can create a Sum object that represents Z. Then we can use a sample from Z to approximate CDF_Z.

This approach is simple and versatile, but not very efficient; we have to generate a large sample to estimate CDF_Z accurately, and even then it is not exact.

If CDF_X and CDF_Y are expressed as functions, sometimes we can find CDF_Z exactly. Here's how:

1. To start, assume that the particular value of X is x. Then $CDF_Z(z)$ is

$$P(Z \leq z \mid X = x) = P(Y \leq z - x)$$

   Let's read that back. The left side is "the probability that the sum is less than z, given that the first term is x." Well, if the first term is x and the sum has to be less than z, then the second term has to be less than $z - x$.

2. To get the probability that Y is less than $z - x$, we evaluate CDF_Y.

$$P(Y \leq z - x) = CDF_Y(z - x)$$

This follows from the definition of the CDF.

3. Good so far? Let's go on. Since we don't actually know the value of x, we have to consider all values it could have and integrate over them:

$$P(Z \leq z) = \int_{-\infty}^{\infty} P(Z \leq z \mid X = x) \, \text{PDF}_X(x) \, dx$$

The integrand is "the probability that Z is less than or equal to z, given that $X = x$, times the probability that $X = x$."

Substituting from the previous steps we get

$$P(Z \leq z) = \int_{-\infty}^{\infty} \text{CDF}_Y(z - x) \, \text{PDF}_X(x) \, dx$$

The left side is the definition of CDF_Z, so we conclude:

$$\text{CDF}_Z(z) = \int_{-\infty}^{\infty} \text{CDF}_Y(z - x) \, \text{PDF}_X(x) \, dx$$

4. To get PDF_Z, take the derivative of both sides with respect to z. The result is

$$\text{PDF}_Z(z) = \int_{-\infty}^{\infty} \text{PDF}_Y(z - x) \, \text{PDF}_X(x) \, dx$$

If you have studied signals and systems, you might recognize that integral. It is the **convolution** of PDF_Y and PDF_X, denoted with the operator $*$.

$$\text{PDF}_Z = \text{PDF}_Y * \text{PDF}_X$$

So the distribution of the sum is the convolution of the distributions. See *http:// wiktionary.org/wiki/booyah*!

As an example, suppose X and Y are random variables with an exponential distribution with parameter λ. The distribution of $Z = X + Y$ is:

$$\text{PDF}_Z(z) = \int_{-\infty}^{\infty} \text{PDF}_X(x) \, \text{PDF}_Y(z - x) \, dx = \int_{-\infty}^{\infty} \lambda e^{-\lambda x} \, \lambda e^{\lambda(z-x)}$$

Now we have to remember that PDF_{expo} is 0 for all negative values, but we can handle that by adjusting the limits of integration:

$$\text{PDF}_Z(z) = \int_{0}^{z} \lambda e^{-\lambda x} \, \lambda e^{-\lambda(z-x)} \, dx$$

Now we can combine terms and move constants outside the integral:

$$\text{PDF}_Z(z) = \lambda^2 e^{-\lambda z} \int_{0}^{z} dx = \lambda^2 z \, e^{-\lambda z}$$

This, it turns out, is the PDF of an Erlang distribution with parameter $k = 2$ (see *http://wikipedia.org/wiki/Erlang_distribution*). So the convolution of two exponential distributions (with the same parameter) is an Erlang distribution.

Exercise 6-7.

If X has an exponential distribution with parameter λ, and Y has an Erlang distribution with parameters k and λ, what is the distribution of the sum $Z = X + Y$?

Exercise 6-8.

Suppose I draw two values from a distribution; what is the distribution of the larger value? Express your answer in terms of the PDF or CDF of the distribution.

As the number of values increases, the distribution of the maximum converges on one of the extreme value distributions; see *http://wikipedia.org/wiki/Gumbel_distribution*.

Exercise 6-9.

If you are given Pmf objects, you can compute the distribution of the sum by enumerating all pairs of values:

```
for x in pmf_x.Values():
    for y in pmf_y.Values():
        z = x + y
```

Write a function that takes PMF_X and PMF_Y and returns a new Pmf that represents the distribution of the sum $Z = X + Y$.

Write a similar function that computes the PMF of $Z = \max(X, Y)$.

Why Normal?

I said earlier that normal distributions are amenable to analysis, but I didn't say why. One reason is that they are closed under linear transformation and convolution. To explain what that means, it will help to introduce some notation.

If the distribution of a random variable, X, is normal with parameters μ and σ, you can write

$$X \sim \mathcal{N}(\mu, \sigma)$$

where the symbol $\sim$ means "is distributed" and the script letter $\mathcal{N}$ stands for "normal."

A linear transformation of X is something like $X' = aX + b$, where a and b are real numbers. A family of distributions is closed under linear transformation if X' is in the same family as X. The normal distribution has this property; if $X \sim \mathcal{N}(\mu, \sigma^2)$,

$$X' \sim \mathcal{N}(a\mu + b, a^2 \sigma^2)$$

Normal distributions are also closed under convolution. If $Z = X + Y$ and $X \sim \mathcal{N}(\mu_X, \sigma_X^2)$ and $Y \sim \mathcal{N}(\mu_Y, \sigma_Y^2)$ then

$$Z \sim (\mu_X + \mu_Y, \sigma_X^2 + \sigma_Y^2)$$

The other distributions we have looked at do not have these properties.

Exercise 6-10.

If $X \sim \mathcal{N}(\mu_X, \sigma_X{}^2)$ and $Y \sim \mathcal{N}(\mu_Y, \sigma_Y{}^2)$, what is the distribution of $Z = aX + bY$?

Exercise 6-11.

Let's see what happens when we add values from other distributions. Choose a pair of distributions (any two of exponential, normal, lognormal, and Pareto) and choose parameters that make their mean and variance similar.

Generate random numbers from these distributions and compute the distribution of their sums. Use the tests from Chapter 4 to see if the sum can be modeled by a continuous distribution.

Central Limit Theorem

So far we have seen:

- If we add values drawn from normal distributions, the distribution of the sum is normal.
- If we add values drawn from other distributions, the sum does not generally have one of the continuous distributions we have seen.

But it turns out that if we add up a large number of values from almost any distribution, the distribution of the sum converges to normal.

More specifically, if the distribution of the values has mean and standard deviation μ and σ, the distribution of the sum is approximately $\mathcal{N}(n\mu, n\sigma^2)$.

This is called the *Central Limit Theorem*. It is one of the most useful tools for statistical analysis, but it comes with caveats:

- The values have to be drawn independently.
- The values have to come from the same distribution (although this requirement can be relaxed).
- The values have to be drawn from a distribution with finite mean and variance, so most Pareto distributions are out.
- The number of values you need before you see convergence depends on the skewness of the distribution. Sums from an exponential distribution converge for small sample sizes. Sums from a lognormal distribution do not.

The Central Limit Theorem explains, at least in part, the prevalence of normal distributions in the natural world. Most characteristics of animals and other life forms are affected by a large number of genetic and environmental factors whose effect is additive.

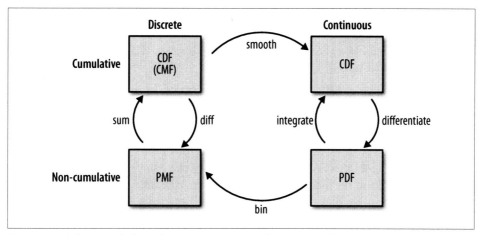

Figure 6-1. A framework that relates representations of distribution functions

The characteristics we measure are the sum of a large number of small effects, so their distribution tends to be normal.

Exercise 6-12.

If I draw a sample, $x_1 .. x_n$, independently from a distribution with finite mean μ and variance σ^2, what is the distribution of the sample mean:

$$\bar{x} = \frac{1}{n} \sum x_i$$

As n increases, what happens to the variance of the sample mean? Hint: review "Why Normal?" on page 67.

Exercise 6-13.

Choose a distribution (one of exponential, lognormal, or Pareto) and choose values for the parameter(s). Generate samples with sizes 2, 4, 8, etc., and compute the distribution of their sums. Use a normal probability plot to see if the distribution is approximately normal. How many terms do you have to add to see convergence?

Exercise 6-14.

Instead of the distribution of sums, compute the distribution of products; what happens as the number of terms increases? Hint: look at the distribution of the log of the products.

The Distribution Framework

At this point, we have seen PMFs, CDFs, and PDFs; let's take a minute to review. Figure 6-1 shows how these functions relate to each other.

We started with PMFs, which represent the probabilities for a discrete set of values. To get from a PMF to a CDF, we computed a cumulative sum. To be more consistent, a discrete CDF should be called a cumulative mass function (CMF), but as far as I can tell no one uses that term.

To get from a CDF to a PMF, you can compute differences in cumulative probabilities.

Similarly, a PDF is the derivative of a continuous CDF; or, equivalently, a CDF is the integral of a PDF. But remember that a PDF maps from values to probability densities; to get a probability, you have to integrate.

To get from a discrete to a continuous distribution, you can perform various kinds of smoothing. One form of smoothing is to assume that the data come from an analytic continuous distribution (like exponential or normal) and to estimate the parameters of that distribution. And that's what Chapter 8 is about.

If you divide a PDF into a set of bins, you can generate a PMF that is at least an approximation of the PDF. We use this technique in Chapter 8 to do Bayesian estimation.

Exercise 6-15.

Write a function called `MakePmfFromCdf` that takes a Cdf object and returns the corresponding Pmf object.

You can find a solution to this exercise in *http://thinkstats.com/Pmf.py*.

Glossary

Central Limit Theorem
> "The supreme law of Unreason," according to Sir Francis Galton, an early statistician.

convolution
> An operation that computes the distribution of the sum of values from two distributions.

illusory superiority
> The tendency of people to imagine that they are better than average.

probability density function (PDF)
> The derivative of a continuous CDF.

random variable
> An object that represents a random process.

random variate
> A value generated by a random process.

robust
> A statistic is robust if it is relatively immune to the effect of outliers.

skewness

A characteristic of a distribution; intuitively, it is a measure of how asymmetric the distribution is.

CHAPTER 7

Hypothesis Testing

Exploring the data from the NSFG, we saw several "apparent effects," including a number of differences between first babies and others. So far, we have taken these effects at face value; in this chapter, finally, we put them to the test.

The fundamental question we want to address is whether these effects are real. For example, if we see a difference in the mean pregnancy length for first babies and others, we want to know whether that difference is real, or whether it occurred by chance.

That question turns out to be hard to address directly, so we will proceed in two steps. First we will test whether the effect is *significant*, then we will try to interpret the result as an answer to the original question.

In the context of statistics, "significant" has a technical definition that is different from its use in common language. As defined earlier, an apparent effect is statistically significant if it is unlikely to have occurred by chance.

To make this more precise, we have to answer three questions:

1. What do we mean by "chance"?
2. What do we mean by "unlikely"?
3. What do we mean by "effect"?

All three of these questions are harder than they look. Nevertheless, there is a general structure that people use to test statistical significance:

Null hypothesis
    A model of the system based on the assumption that the apparent effect was actually due to chance.

p-value
    The probability of the apparent effect under the null hypothesis.

Interpretation
    Based on the p-value, we conclude that the effect is either statistically significant, or not.

This process is called *hypothesis testing*. The underlying logic is similar to a proof by contradiction. To prove a mathematical statement, A, you assume temporarily that A is false. If that assumption leads to a contradiction, you conclude that A must actually be true.

Similarly, to test a hypothesis like, "This effect is real," we assume, temporarily, that is is not. That's the null hypothesis. Based on that assumption, we compute the probability of the apparent effect. That's the p-value. If the p-value is low enough, we conclude that the null hypothesis is unlikely to be true.

Testing a Difference in Means

One of the easiest hypotheses to test is an apparent difference in mean between two groups. In the NSFG data, we saw that the mean pregnancy length for first babies is slightly longer, and the mean weight at birth is slightly smaller. Now we will see if those effects are significant.

For these examples, the null hypothesis is that the distributions for the two groups are the same, and that the apparent difference is due to chance.

To compute p-values, we find the pooled distribution for all live births (first babies and others), generate random samples that are the same size as the observed samples, and compute the difference in means under the null hypothesis.

If we generate a large number of samples, we can count how often the difference in means (due to chance) is as big or bigger than the difference we actually observed. This fraction is the p-value.

For pregnancy length, we observed $n = 4{,}413$ first babies and $m = 4{,}735$ others, and the difference in mean was $\delta = 0.078$ weeks. To approximate the p-value of this effect, I pooled the distributions, generated samples with sizes n and m, and computed the difference in mean.

This is another example of resampling, because we are drawing a random sample from a dataset that is, itself, a sample of the general population. I computed differences for 1,000 sample pairs; Figure 7-1 shows their distribution.

The mean difference is near 0, as you would expect with samples from the same distribution. The vertical lines show the cutoffs where $x = -\delta$ or $x = \delta$.

Of 1,000 sample pairs, there were 166 where the difference in mean (positive or negative) was as big or bigger than δ, so the p-value is approximately 0.166. In other words, we expect to see an effect as big as δ about 17% of the time, even if the actual distribution for the two groups is the same.

So the apparent effect is not very likely, but is it unlikely enough? I'll address that in the next section.

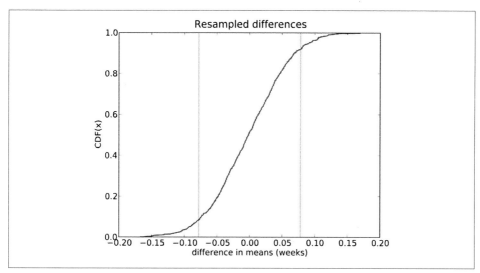

Figure 7-1. CDF of difference in mean for resampled data

Exercise 7-1.

In the NSFG dataset, the difference in mean weight for first births is 2.0 ounces. Compute the p-value of this difference.

Hint: for this kind of resampling it is important to sample with replacement, so you should use `random.choice` rather than `random.sample` (see "Random Numbers" on page 31).

You can start with the code I used to generate the results in this section, which you can download from *http://thinkstats.com/hypothesis.py*.

Choosing a Threshold

In hypothesis testing, we have to worry about two kinds of errors.

- A type I error, also called a *false positive*, is when we accept a hypothesis that is actually false; that is, we consider an effect significant when it was actually due to chance.

- A type II error, also called a *false negative*, is when we reject a hypothesis that is actually true; that is, we attribute an effect to chance when it was actually real.

The most common approach to hypothesis testing is to choose a threshold,[1] α, for the p-value and to accept as significant any effect with a p-value less than α. A common choice for α is 5%. By this criterion, the apparent difference in pregnancy length for first babies is not significant, but the difference in weight is.

---

1. Also known as a "significance criterion."

For this kind of hypothesis testing, we can compute the probability of a false positive explicitly: it turns out to be α.

To see why, think about the definition of false positive—the chance of accepting a hypothesis that is false—and the definition of a p-value—the chance of generating the measured effect if the hypothesis is false.

Putting these together, we can ask: if the hypothesis is false, what is the chance of generating a measured effect that will be considered significant with threshold α? The answer is α.

We can decrease the chance of a false positive by decreasing the threshold. For example, if the threshold is 1%, there is only a 1% chance of a false positive.

But there is a price to pay: decreasing the threshold raises the standard of evidence, which increases the chance of rejecting a valid hypothesis.

In general, there is a trade-off between type I and type II errors. The only way to decrease both at the same time is to increase the sample size (or, in some cases, decrease measurement error).

Exercise 7-2.

To investigate the effect of sample size on p-value, see what happens if you discard half of the data from the NSFG. Hint: use `random.sample`. What if you discard three-quarters of the data, and so on?

What is the smallest sample size where the difference in mean birth weight is still significant with $\alpha = 5\%$? How much larger does the sample size have to be with $\alpha = 1\%$?

You can start with the code I used to generate the results in this section, which you can download from *http://thinkstats.com/hypothesis.py*.

Defining the Effect

When something unusual happens, people often say something like, "Wow! What were the chances of *that*?" This question makes sense because we have an intuitive sense that some things are more likely than others. But this intuition doesn't always hold up to scrutiny.

For example, suppose I toss a coin 10 times, and after each toss I write down H for heads and T for tails. If the result was a sequence like THHTHTTTHH, you wouldn't be too surprised. But if the result was HHHHHHHHHH, you would say something like, "Wow! What were the chances of *that*?"

But in this example, the probability of the two sequences is the same: 1 in 1,024. And the same is true for any other sequence. So when we ask, "What were the chances of *that*," we have to be careful about what we mean by "that."

For the NSFG data, I defined the effect as "a difference in mean (positive or negative) as big or bigger than δ." By making this choice, I decided to evaluate the magnitude of the difference, ignoring the sign.

A test like that is called *two-sided*, because we consider both sides (positive and negative) in the distribution from Figure 7-1. By using a two-sided test, we are testing the hypothesis that there is a significant difference between the distributions, without specifying the sign of the difference.

The alternative is to use a *one-sided* test, which asks whether the mean for first babies is significantly *higher* than the mean for others. Because the hypothesis is more specific, the p-value is lower—in this case it is roughly half.

Interpreting the Result

At the beginning of this chapter, I said that the question we want to address is whether an apparent effect is real. We started by defining the null hypothesis, denoted H_0, which is the hypothesis that the effect is not real. Then we defined the p-value, which is $P(E|H_0)$, where E is an effect as big as or bigger than the apparent effect. Then we computed p-values and compared them to a threshold, α.

That's a useful step, but it doesn't answer the original question, which is whether the effect is real. There are several ways to interpret the result of a hypothesis test:

Classical
> In classical hypothesis testing, if a p-value is less than α, you can say that the effect is statistically significant, but you can't conclude that it's real. This formulation is careful to avoid leaping to conclusions, but it is deeply unsatisfying.

Practical
> In practice, people are not so formal. In most science journals, researchers report p-values without apology, and readers interpret them as evidence that the apparent effect is real. The lower the p-value, the higher their confidence in this conclusion.

Bayesian
> What we really want to know is $P(H_A|E)$, where H_A is the hypothesis that the effect is real. By Bayes's theorem

$$P(H_A \mid E) = \frac{P(E \mid H_A)\, P(H_A)}{P(E)}$$

> where $P(H_A)$ is the prior probability of H_A before we saw the effect, $P(E|H_A)$ is the probability of seeing E, assuming that the effect is real, and $P(E)$ is the probability of seeing E under any hypothesis. Since the effect is either real or it's not,

$$P(E) = P(E|H_A)\, P(H_A) + P(E|H_0)\, P(H_0)$$

As an example, I'll compute $P(H_A|E)$ for pregnancy lengths in the NSFG. We have already computed $P(E|H_0) = 0.166$, so all we have to do is compute $P(E|H_A)$ and choose a value for the prior.

To compute $P(E|H_A)$, we assume that the effect is real—that is, that the difference in mean duration, δ, is actually what we observed, 0.078. (This way of formulating H_A is a little bit bogus. I will explain and fix the problem in the next section.)

By generating 1,000 sample pairs, one from each distribution, I estimated $P(E|H_A) = 0.494$. With the prior $P(H_A) = 0.5$, the posterior probability of H_A is 0.748.

So if the prior probability of H_A is 50%, the updated probability, taking into account the evidence from this dataset, is almost 75%. It makes sense that the posterior is higher, since the data provide some support for the hypothesis. But it might seem surprising that the difference is so large, especially since we found that the difference in means was not statistically significant.

In fact, the method I used in this section is not quite right, and it tends to overstate the impact of the evidence. In the next section, we will correct this tendency.

Exercise 7-3.

Using the data from the NSFG, what is the posterior probability that the distribution of birth weights is different for first babies and others?

You can start with the code I used to generate the results in this section, which you can download from *http://thinkstats.com/hypothesis.py*.

Cross-Validation

In the previous example, we used the dataset to formulate the hypothesis H_A, and then we used the same dataset to test it. That's not a good idea; it is too easy to generate misleading results.

The problem is that even when the null hypothesis is true, there is likely to be some difference, δ, between any two groups, just by chance. If we use the observed value of δ to formulate the hypothesis, $P(H_A|E)$ is likely to be high even when H_A is false.

We can address this problem with *cross-validation*, which uses one dataset to compute δ and a *different* dataset to evaluate H_A. The first dataset is called the *training set*; the second is called the *testing set*.

In a study like the NSFG, which studies a different cohort in each cycle, we can use one cycle for training and another for testing. Or we can partition the data into subsets (at random), then use one for training and one for testing.

I implemented the second approach, dividing the Cycle 6 data roughly in half. I ran the test several times with different random partitions. The average posterior probability was $P(H_A|E) = 0.621$. As expected, the impact of the evidence is smaller, partly because of the smaller sample size in the test set, and also because we are no longer using the same data for training and testing.

Reporting Bayesian Probabilities

In the previous section, we chose the prior probability $P(H_A) = 0.5$. If we have a set of hypotheses and no reason to think one is more likely than another, it is common to assign each the same probability.

Some people object to Bayesian probabilities because they depend on prior probabilities, and people might not agree on the right priors. For people who expect scientific results to be objective and universal, this property is deeply unsettling.

One response to this objection is that, in practice, strong evidence tends to swamp the effect of the prior, so people who start with different priors will converge toward the same posterior probability.

Another option is to report just the *likelihood ratio*, $P(E \mid H_A)$ / $P(E|H_0)$, rather than the posterior probability. That way, readers can plug in whatever prior they like and compute their own posteriors (no pun intended). The likelihood ratio is sometimes called a Bayes factor (see *http://wikipedia.org/wiki/Bayes_factor*).

Exercise 7-4.

If your prior probability for a hypothesis, H_A, is 0.3 and new evidence becomes available that yields a likelihood ratio of 3 relative to the null hypothesis, H_0, what is your posterior probability for H_A?

Exercise 7-5.

This exercise is adapted from MacKay, *Information Theory, Inference, and Learning Algorithms*:

> Two people have left traces of their own blood at the scene of a crime. A suspect, Oliver, is tested and found to have type O blood. The blood groups of the two traces are found to be of type O (a common type in the local population, having frequency 60%) and of type AB (a rare type, with frequency 1%). Do these data (the blood types found at the scene) give evidence in favor of the proposition that Oliver was one of the two people whose blood was found at the scene?

Hint: Compute the likelihood ratio for this evidence; if it is greater than 1, then the evidence is in favor of the proposition. For a solution and discussion, see page 55 of MacKay's book.

Chi-Square Test

In "Choosing a Threshold" on page 75 we concluded that the apparent difference in mean pregnancy length for first babies and others was not significant. But in "Relative Risk" on page 19, when we computed relative risk, we saw that first babies are more likely to be early, less likely to be on time, and more likely to be late.

So maybe the distributions have the same mean and different variance. We could test the significance of the difference in variance, but variances are less robust than means, and hypothesis tests for variance often behave badly.

An alternative is to test a hypothesis that more directly reflects the effect as it appears; that is, the hypothesis that first babies are more likely to be early, less likely to be on time, and more likely to be late.

We proceed in five easy steps:

1. We define a set of categories, called *cells*, that each baby might fall into. In this example, there are six cells because there are two groups (first babies and others) and three bins (early, on time, or late).

   I'll use the definitions from "Relative Risk" on page 19: a baby is early if it is born during Week 37 or earlier, on time if it is born during Week 38, 39, or 40, and late if it is born during Week 41 or later.

2. We compute the number of babies we expect in each cell. Under the null hypothesis, we assume that the distributions are the same for the two groups, so we can compute the pooled probabilities: P(early), P(ontime), and P(late).

   For first babies, we have $n = 4,413$ samples, so under the null hypothesis we expect n P(early) first babies to be early, n P(ontime) to be on time, etc. Likewise, we have $m = 4,735$ other babies, so we expect m P(early) other babies to be early, etc.

3. For each cell we compute the deviation; that is, the difference between the observed value, O_i, and the expected value, E_i.

4. We compute some measure of the total deviation; this quantity is called the *test statistic*. The most common choice is the chi-square statistic:

$$\chi^2 = \sum_i \frac{(O_i - E_i)^2}{E_i}$$

5. We can use a Monte Carlo simulation to compute the p-value, which is the probability of seeing a chi-square statistic as high as the observed value under the null hypothesis.

When the chi-square statistic is used, this process is called a *chi-square test*. One feature of the chi-square test is that the distribution of the test statistic can be computed analytically.

Using the data from the NSFG, I computed $\chi^2 = 91.64$, which would occur by chance about one time in 10,000. I conclude that this result is statistically significant, with one caution: again we used the same dataset for exploration and testing. It would be a good idea to confirm this result with another dataset.

You can download the code I used in this section from *http://thinkstats.com/chi.py*.

Exercise 7-6.

Suppose you run a casino and you suspect that a customer has replaced a die provided by the casino with a "crooked die"; that is, one that has been tampered with to make one of the faces more likely to come up than the others. You apprehend the alleged cheater and confiscate the die, but now you have to prove that it is crooked.

You roll the die 60 times and get the following results:

Value	1	2	3	4	5	6
Frequency	8	9	19	6	8	10

What is the chi-squared statistic for these values? What is the probability of seeing a chi-squared value as large by chance?

Efficient Resampling

Anyone reading this book who has prior training in statistics probably laughed when they saw Figure 7-1, because I used a lot of computer power to simulate something I could have figured out analytically.

Obviously, mathematical analysis is not the focus of this book. I am willing to use computers to do things the "dumb" way, because I think it is easier for beginners to understand simulations, and easier to demonstrate that they are correct. So as long as the simulations don't take too long to run, I don't feel guilty for skipping the analysis.

However, there are times when a little analysis can save a lot of computing, and Figure 7-1 is one of those times.

Remember that we were testing the observed difference in the mean between pregnancy lengths for $n = 4,413$ first babies and $m = 4,735$ others. We formed the pooled distribution for all babies, drew samples with sizes n and m, and computed the difference in sample means.

Instead, we could directly compute the distribution of the difference in sample means. To get started, let's think about what a sample mean is: we draw n samples from a distribution, add them up, and divide by n. If the distribution has mean μ and variance σ^2, then by the Central Limit Theorem, we know that the sum of the samples is $\mathcal{N}(n\mu, n\sigma^2)$.

To figure out the distribution of the sample means, we have to invoke one of the properties of the normal distribution: if X is $\mathcal{N}(\mu, \sigma^2)$,

$$aX + b \sim \mathcal{N}(a\mu + b, a^2 \sigma^2)$$

When we divide by n, $a = 1/n$ and $b = 0$, so

$$X/n \sim \mathcal{N}(\mu/n, \sigma^2/n^2)$$

So the distribution of the sample mean is $\mathcal{N}(\mu, \sigma^2/n)$.

To get the distribution of the difference between two sample means, we invoke another property of the normal distribution: if X_1 is $\mathcal{N}(\mu_1, \sigma_1^2)$ and X_2 is $\mathcal{N}(\mu_2, \sigma_2^2)$,

$$aX_1 + bX_2 \sim (a\mu_1 + b\mu_2, a^2\sigma_1^2 + b^2\sigma_2^2)$$

So as a special case:

$$X_1 - X_2 \sim (\mu_1 - \mu_2, \sigma_1^2 + \sigma_2^2)$$

Putting it all together, we conclude that the sample in Figure 7-1 is drawn from $\mathcal{N}(0, f\sigma^2)$, where $f = 1/n + 1/m$. Plugging in $n = 4413$ and $m = 4735$, we expect the difference of sample means to be $\mathcal{N}(0, 0.0032)$.

We can use `erf.NormalCdf` to compute the p-value of the observed difference in the means:

```
delta = 0.078
sigma = math.sqrt(0.0032)
left = erf.NormalCdf(-delta, 0.0, sigma)
right = 1 - erf.NormalCdf(delta, 0.0, sigma)
```

The sum of the left and right tails is the p-value, 0.168, which is pretty close to what we estimated by resampling, 0.166. You can download the code I used in this section from *http://thinkstats.com/hypothesis_analytic.py*.

Power

When the result of a hypothesis test is negative (that is, the effect is not statistically significant), can we conclude that the effect is not real? That depends on the power of the test.

Statistical *power* is the probability that the test will be positive if the null hypothesis is false. In general, the power of a test depends on the sample size, the magnitude of the effect, and the threshold α.

Exercise 7-7.

What is the power of the test in "Choosing a Threshold" on page 75, using $\alpha = 0.05$ and assuming that the actual difference between the means is 0.078 weeks?

You can estimate power by generating random samples from distributions with the given difference in the mean, testing the observed difference in the mean, and counting the number of positive tests.

What is the power of the test with $\alpha = 0.10$?

One way to report the power of a test, along with a negative result, is to say something like, "If the apparent effect were as large as x, this test would reject the null hypothesis with probability p."

Glossary

cell
> In a chi-square test, the categories the observations are divided into.

chi-square test
> A test that uses the chi-square statistic as the test statistic.

cross-validation
> A process of hypothesis testing that uses one dataset for exploratory data analysis and another dataset for testing.

false negative
> The conclusion that an effect is due to chance when it is not.

false positive
> The conclusion that an effect is real when it is not.

hypothesis testing
> The process of determining whether an apparent effect is statistically significant.

likelihood ratio
> The ratio of $P(E|A)$ to $P(E|B)$ for two hypotheses A and B, which is a way to report results from a Bayesian analysis without depending on priors.

null hypothesis
> A model of a system based on the assumption that an apparent effect is due to chance.

one-sided test
> A test that asks, "What is the chance of an effect as big as the observed effect, and with the same sign?"

p-value
> The probability that an effect could occur by chance.

power
> The probability that a test will reject the null hypothesis if it is false.

significant
> An effect is statistically significant if it is unlikely to occur by chance.

test statistic
> A statistic used to measure the deviation of an apparent effect from what is expected by chance.

testing set
> A dataset used for testing.

training set
> A dataset used to formulate a hypothesis for testing.

two-sided test
> A test that asks, "What is the chance of an effect as big as the observed effect, positive or negative?"

CHAPTER 8

Estimation

The Estimation Game

Let's play a game. I'll think of a distribution, and you have to guess what it is. We'll start out easy and work our way up.

I'm thinking of a distribution. I'll give you two hints; it's a normal distribution, and here's a random sample drawn from it:

{-0.441, 1.774, -0.101, -1.138, 2.975, -2.138}

What do you think is the mean parameter, μ, of this distribution?

One choice is to use the sample mean to estimate μ. Up until now, we have used the symbol μ for both the sample mean and the mean parameter, but now to distinguish them I will use $\bar{x}$ for the sample mean. In this example, $\bar{x}$ is 0.155, so it would be reasonable to guess $\mu = 0.155$.

This process is called *estimation*, and the statistic we used (the sample mean) is called an *estimator*.

Using the sample mean to estimate μ is so obvious that it is hard to imagine a reasonable alternative. But suppose we change the game by introducing outliers.

I'm thinking of a distribution. It's a normal distribution, and here's a sample that was collected by an unreliable surveyor who occasionally puts the decimal point in the wrong place.

{-0.441, 1.774, -0.101, -1.138, 2.975, -213.8}

Now what's your estimate of μ? If you use the sample mean, your guess is -35.12. Is that the best choice? What are the alternatives?

One option is to identify and discard outliers, then compute the sample mean of the rest. Another option is to use the median as an estimator.

Which estimator is the best depends on the circumstances (for example, whether there are outliers) and on what the goal is. Are you trying to minimize errors, or maximize your chance of getting the right answer?

If there are no outliers, the sample mean minimizes the *mean squared error*, or MSE. If we play the game many times, and each time compute the error $\bar{x} - \mu$, the sample mean minimizes

$$MSE = \frac{1}{m} \sum (\bar{x} - \mu)^2$$

Where m is the number of times you play the estimation game (not to be confused with n, which is the size of the sample used to compute $\bar{x}$).

Minimizing MSE is a nice property, but it's not always the best strategy. For example, suppose we are estimating the distribution of wind speeds at a building site. If we guess too high, we might overbuild the structure, increasing its cost. But if we guess too low, the building might collapse. Because cost as a function of error is asymmetric, minimizing MSE is not the best strategy.

As another example, suppose I roll three six-sided dice and ask you to predict the total. If you get it exactly right, you get a prize; otherwise, you get nothing. In this case, the value that minimizes MSE is 10.5, but that would be a terrible guess. For this game, you want an estimator that has the highest chance of being right, which is a *maximum likelihood estimator*, or MLE. If you pick 10 or 11, your chance of winning is 1 in 8, and that's the best you can do.

Exercise 8-1.

Write a function that draws six values from a normal distribution with $\mu = 0$ and $\sigma = 1$. Use the sample mean to estimate μ and compute the error $\bar{x} - \mu$. Run the function 1,000 times and compute MSE.

Now modify the program to use the median as an estimator. Compute MSE again and compare to the MSE for $\bar{x}$.

Guess the Variance

I'm thinking of a distribution. It's a normal distribution, and here's a (familiar) sample:

{-0.441, 1.774, -0.101, -1.138, 2.975, -2.138}

What do you think is the variance, σ^2, of my distribution? Again, the obvious choice is to use the sample variance as an estimator. I will use S^2 to denote the sample variance, to distinguish from the unknown parameter σ^2.

$$S^2 = \frac{1}{n} \sum (x_i - \bar{x})^2$$

For large samples, S^2 is an adequate estimator, but for small samples it tends to be too low. Because of this unfortunate property, it is called a *biased* estimator.

An estimator is *unbiased* if the expected total (or mean) error, after many iterations of the estimation game, is 0. Fortunately, there is another simple statistic that is an unbiased estimator of σ^2:

$$S_{n-1}^2 = \frac{1}{n-1} \sum (x_i - \bar{x})^2$$

The biggest problem with this estimator is that its name and symbol are used inconsistently. The name "sample variance" can refer to either S^2 or S_{n-1}^2 and the symbol S^2 is used for either or both.

For an explanation of why S^2 is biased, and a proof that S_{n-1}^2 is unbiased, see *http://wikipedia.org/wiki/Bias_of_an_estimator*.

Exercise 8-2.

Write a function that draws six values from a normal distribution with $\mu = 0$ and $\sigma = 1$. Use the sample variance to estimate σ^2 and compute the error $S^2 - \sigma^2$. Run the function 1,000 times and compute mean error (not squared).

Now modify the program to use the unbiased estimator S_{n-1}^2. Compute the mean error again and see if it converges to zero as you increase the number of games.

Understanding Errors

Before we go on, let's clear up a common source of confusion. Properties like MSE and bias are long-term expectations based on many iterations of the estimation game.

While you are playing the game, you don't know the errors. That is, if I give you a sample and ask you to estimate a parameter, you can compute the value of the estimator, but you can't compute the error. If you could, you wouldn't need the estimator!

The reason we talk about estimation error is to describe the behavior of different estimators in the long run. In this chapter we run experiments to examine those behaviors; these experiments are artificial in the sense that we know the actual values of the parameters, so we can compute errors. But when you work with real data, you don't, so you can't.

Now let's get back to the game.

Exponential Distributions

I'm thinking of a distribution. It's an exponential distribution, and here's a sample:

{5.384, 4.493, 19.198, 2.790, 6.122, 12.844}

What do you think is the parameter, λ, of this distribution?

In general, the mean of an exponential distribution is $1/\lambda$, so working backwards, we might choose

$$\hat{\lambda} = 1 / \bar{x}$$

It is common to use hat notation for estimators, so $\hat{\lambda}$ is an estimator of λ. And not just any estimator; it is also the MLE estimator.[1] So if you want to maximize your chance of guessing λ exactly, $\hat{\lambda}$ is the way to go.

But we know that $\bar{x}$ is not robust in the presence of outliers, so we expect $\hat{\lambda}$ to have the same problem.

Maybe we can find an alternative based on the sample median. Remember that the median of an exponential distribution is $\log(2) / \lambda$, so working backwards again, we can define an estimator

$$\hat{\lambda}_{1/2} = \log(2) / \mu_{1/2}$$

where $\mu_{1/2}$ is the sample median.

Exercise 8-3.
Run an experiment to see which of $\hat{\lambda}$ and $\hat{\lambda}_{1/2}$ yields lower MSE. Test whether either of them is biased.

Confidence Intervals

So far, we have looked at estimators that generate single values, known as *point estimates*. For many problems, we might prefer an interval that specifies an upper and lower bound on the unknown parameter.

Or, more generally, we might want that whole distribution; that is, the range of values the parameter could have, and for each value in the range, a notion of how likely it is.

Let's start with *confidence intervals*.

I'm thinking of a distribution. It's an exponential distribution, and here's a sample:

{5.384, 4.493, 19.198, 2.790, 6.122, 12.844}

---

1. See *http://wikipedia.org/wiki/Exponential_distribution#Maximum_likelihood*.

I want you to give me a range of values that you think is likely to contain the unknown parameter λ. More specifically, I want a 90% confidence interval, which means that if we play this game over and over, your interval will contain λ 90% of the time.

It turns out that this version of the game is hard, so I'm going to tell you the answer, and all you have to do is test it.

Confidence intervals are usually described in terms of the miss rate, α, so a 90% confidence interval has miss rate $\alpha = 0.1$. The confidence interval for the λ parameter of an exponential distribution is

$$\left(\hat{\lambda} \frac{\chi^2(2n, 1 - \alpha/2)}{2n}, \hat{\lambda} \frac{\chi^2(2n, \alpha/2)}{2n} \right)$$

where n is the sample size, $\hat{\lambda}$ is the mean-based estimator from the previous section, and $\chi^2(k, x)$ is the CDF of a chi-squared distribution with k degrees of freedom, evaluated at x (see *http://wikipedia.org/wiki/Chi-square_distribution*).

In general, confidence intervals are hard to compute analytically, but relatively easy to estimate using simulation. But first we need to talk about Bayesian estimation.

Bayesian Estimation

If you collect a sample and compute a 90% confidence interval, it is tempting to say that the true value of the parameter has a 90% chance of falling in the interval. But from a frequentist point of view, that is not correct because the parameter is an unknown but fixed value. It is either in the interval you computed or not, so the frequentist definition of probability doesn't apply.

So let's try a different version of the game.

I'm thinking of a distribution. It's an exponential distribution, and I chose λ from a uniform distribution between 0.5 and 1.5. Here's a sample, which I'll call X:

{2.675, 0.198, 1.152, 0.787, 2.717, 4.269}

Based on this sample, what value of λ do you think I chose?

In this version of the game, λ *is* a random quantity, so we can reasonably talk about its distribution, and we can compute it easily using Bayes's theorem.

Here are the steps:

1. Divide the range (0.5, 1.5) into a set of equal-sized bins. For each bin, we define H_i, which is the hypothesis that the actual value of λ falls in the i th bin. Since λ was drawn from a uniform distribution, the prior probability, $P(H_i)$, is the same for all i.

2. For each hypothesis, we compute the likelihood, $P(X|H_i)$, which is the chance of drawing the sample X given H_i.

$$P(X \mid H_i) = \prod_j \text{expo}(\lambda_i, x_j)$$

where expo(λ, x) is a function that computes the PDF of the exponential distribution with parameter λ, evaluated at x.

$$PDF_{expo}(\lambda, x) = \lambda e^{-\lambda x}$$

The symbol Π represents the product of a sequence (see *http://wikipedia.org/wiki/Multiplication#Capital_Pi_notation*).

3. Then by Bayes's theorem the posterior distribution is

$$P(H_i|X) = P(H_i)\, P(X|H_i)\, /f$$

where f is the normalization factor

$$f = \sum_i P(H_i)P(X \mid H_i)$$

Given a posterior distribution, it is easy to compute a confidence interval. For example, to compute a 90% CI, you can use the 5th and 95th percentiles of the posterior.

Bayesian confidence intervals are sometimes called *credible intervals*; for a discussion of the differences, see *http://wikipedia.org/wiki/Credible_interval*.

Implementing Bayesian Estimation

To represent the prior distribution, we could use a Pmf, Cdf, or any other representation of a distribution, but since we want to map from a hypothesis to a probability, a Pmf is a natural choice.

Each value in the Pmf represents a hypothesis; for example, the value 0.5 represents the hypothesis that λ is 0.5. In the prior distribution, all hypotheses have the same probability. So we can construct the prior like this:

```
def MakeUniformSuite(low, high, steps):
    hypos = [low + (high-low) * i / (steps-1.0) for i in range(steps)]
    pmf = Pmf.MakePmfFromList(hypos)
    return pmf
```

This function makes and returns a Pmf that represents a collection of related hypotheses, called a *suite*. Each hypothesis has the same probability, so the distribution is *uniform*.

The arguments low and high specify the range of values; steps is the number of hypotheses.

To perform the update, we take a suite of hypotheses and a body of evidence:

```
def Update(suite, evidence):
    for hypo in suite.Values():
        likelihood = Likelihood(evidence, hypo)
        suite.Mult(hypo, likelihood)
    suite.Normalize()
```

For each hypothesis in the suite, we multiply the prior probability by the likelihood of the evidence. Then we normalize the suite.

In this function, suite has to be a Pmf, but evidence can be any type, as long as Likelihood knows how to interpret it.

Here's the likelihood function:

```
def Likelihood(evidence, hypo):
    param = hypo
    likelihood = 1
    for x in evidence:
        likelihood *= ExpoPdf(x, param)

    return likelihood
```

In Likelihood, we assume that evidence is a sample from an exponential distribution and compute the product in the previous section.

ExpoPdf evaluates the PDF of the exponential distribution at x:

```
def ExpoPdf(x, param):
    p = param * math.exp(-param * x)
    return p
```

Putting it all together, here's the code that creates the prior and computes the posterior:

```
evidence = [2.675, 0.198, 1.152, 0.787, 2.717, 4.269]
prior = MakeUniformSuite(0.5, 1.5, 100)
posterior = prior.Copy()
Update(posterior, evidence)
```

You can download the code in this section from *http://thinkstats.com/estimate.py*.

When I think of Bayesian estimation, I imagine a room full of people, where each person has a different guess about whatever you are trying to estimate. So in this example they each have a guess about the correct value of λ.

Initially, each person has a degree of confidence about their own hypothesis. After seeing the evidence, each person updates their confidence based on $P(E|H)$, the likelihood of the evidence, given their hypothesis.

Most often, the likelihood function computes a probability, which is at most 1, so initially everyone's confidence goes down (or stays the same). But then we normalize, which increases everyone's confidence.

So the net effect is that some people get more confident, and some less, depending on the relative likelihood of their hypothesis.

Censored Data

The following problem appears in Chapter 3 of David MacKay's *Information Theory, Inference and Learning Algorithms*, which you can download from *http://www.inference .phy.cam.ac.uk/mackay/itprnn/ps/*.

> Unstable particles are emitted from a source and decay at a distance x, a real number that has an exponential probability distribution with [parameter] λ. Decay events can only be observed if they occur in a window extending from $x = 1$ cm to $x = 20$ cm. n decays are observed at locations $\{x_1, \dots, x_N\}$. What is λ?

This is an example of an estimation problem with *censored data*; that is, we know that some data is systematically excluded.

One of the strengths of Bayesian estimation is that it can deal with censored data with relative ease. We can use the method from the previous section with only one change: we have to replace PDF_{expo} with the conditional distribution:

$$\text{PDF}_{cond}(\lambda, x) = \lambda e^{-\lambda x}/Z(\lambda)$$

for $1 < x < 20$, and 0 otherwise, with

$$Z(\lambda) = \int_1^{20} \lambda e^{-\lambda x}\, dx = e^{-\lambda} - e^{-20\lambda}$$

You might remember $Z(\lambda)$ from Exercise 6-5. I told you to keep it handy.

Exercise 8-4.

Download *http://thinkstats.com/estimate.py*, which contains the code from the previous section, and make a copy named `decay.py`.

Modify `decay.py` to compute the posterior distribution of λ for the sample X = {1.5, 2, 3, 4, 5, 12}. For the prior, you can use a uniform distribution between 0 and 1.5 (not including 0).

You can download a solution to this problem from *http://thinkstats.com/decay.py*.

Exercise 8-5.

In the 2008 Minnesota Senate race, the final vote count was 1,212,629 votes for Al Franken and 1,212,317 votes for Norm Coleman. Franken was declared the winner, but as Charles Seife points out in *Proofiness*, the margin of victory was much smaller than the margin of error, so the result should have been considered a tie.

Assuming that there is a chance that any vote might be lost and a chance that any vote might be double-counted, what is the probability that Coleman actually received more votes?

Hint: you will have to fill in some details to model the error process.

The Locomotive Problem

The locomotive problem is a classic estimation problem also known as the "German tank problem." Here is the version that appears in Mosteller, *Fifty Challenging Problems in Probability*:

> A railroad numbers its locomotives in order 1..N. One day you see a locomotive with the number 60. Estimate how many locomotives the railroad has.

Before you read the rest of this section, try to answer these questions:

1. For a given estimate, $\hat{N}$, what is the likelihood of the evidence, $P(E|\hat{N})$? What is the maximum likelihood estimator?

2. If we see train i it seems reasonable that we would guess some multiple of i so let's assume $\hat{N} = ai$. What value of a minimizes mean squared error?

3. Still assuming that $\hat{N} = ai$ can you find a value of a that makes $\hat{N}$ an unbiased estimator?

4. For what value of N is 60 the average value?

5. What is the Bayesian posterior distribution assuming a prior distribution that is uniform from 1 to 200?

For best results, you should take some time to work on these questions before you continue.

For a given estimate, $\hat{N}$, the likelihood of seeing train i is $1/\hat{N}$ if $i \le \hat{N}$, and 0 otherwise. So the MLE is $\hat{N} = i$. In other words, if you see train 60 and you want to maximize your chance of getting the answer exactly right, you should guess that there are 60 trains.

But this estimator doesn't do very well in terms of MSE. We can do better by choosing $\hat{N} = ai$; all we have to do is find a good value for a.

Suppose that there are, in fact, N trains. Each time we play the estimation game, we see train i and guess ai, so the squared error is $(ai - N)^2$.

If we play the game N times and see each train once, the mean squared error is

$$MSE = \frac{1}{N} \sum_{i=1}^{N} (ai - N)^2$$

To minimize MSE, we take the derivative with respect to a:

$$\frac{dMSE}{da} = \frac{1}{N} \sum_{i=1}^{N} 2i(ai - N) = 0$$

And solve for a.

$$a = \frac{3N}{2N+1}$$

At first glance, that doesn't seem very useful, because N appears on the right-hand side, which suggests that we need to know N to choose a, but if we knew N, we wouldn't need an estimator in the first place.

However, for large values of N, the optimal value for a converges to 3/2, so we could choose $\hat{N} = 3i/2$.

To find an unbiased estimator, we can compute the mean error (ME):

$$ME = \frac{1}{N}\sum_{i=1}^{N}(ai - N)$$

And find the value of a that yields ME = 0, which turns out to be

$$a = \frac{2N}{N-1}$$

For large values of N, a converges to 2, so we could choose $\hat{N} = 2i$.

So far, we have generated three estimators, i, $3i/2$, and $2i$, that have the properties of maximizing likelihood, minimizing squared error, and being unbiased.

Yet another way to generate an estimator is to choose the value that makes the population mean equal the sample mean. If we see train i, the sample mean is just i; the train population that has the same mean is $\hat{N} = 2i - 1$.

Finally, to compute the Bayesian posterior distribution, we compute

$$P(H_n \mid i) = \frac{P(i \mid H_n)P(H_n)}{P(i)}$$

Where H_n is the hypothesis that there are n trains, and i is the evidence: we saw train i. Again, $P(i|H_n)$ is $1/n$ if $i < n$, and 0 otherwise. The normalizing constant, $P(i)$, is just the sum of the numerators for each hypothesis.

If the prior distribution is uniform from 1 to 200, we start with 200 hypotheses and compute the likelihood for each. You can download an implementation from *http://thinkstats.com/locomotive.py*. Figure 8-1 shows what the result looks like.

The 90% credible interval for this posterior is [63, 189], which is still quite wide. Seeing one train doesn't provide strong evidence for any of the hypotheses (although it does rule out the hypotheses with $n < i$).

If we start with a different prior, the posterior is significantly different, which helps to explain why the other estimators are so diverse.

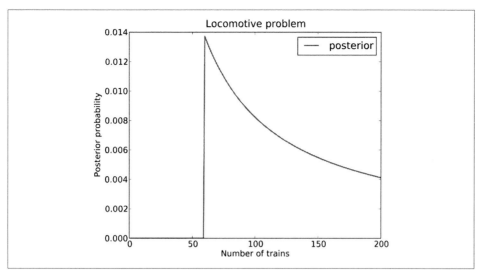

Figure 8-1. Posterior distribution of the number of trains

One way to think of different estimators is that they are implicitly based on different priors. If there is enough evidence to swamp the priors, then all estimators tend to converge; otherwise, as in this case, there is no single estimator that has all of the properties we might want.

Exercise 8-6.

Generalize `locomotive.py` to handle the case where you see more than one train. You should only have to change a few lines of code.

See if you can answer the other questions for the case where you see more than one train. You can find a discussion of the problem and several solutions at *http://wikipedia .org/wiki/German_tank_problem.*

Glossary

bias

The tendency of an estimator to be above or below the actual value of the parameter, when averaged over repeated samples.

censored data

A dataset sampled in a way that systematically excludes some data.

confidence interval

An estimate expressed as an interval with a given probability of containing the true value of the parameter.

credible interval

Another name for a Bayesian confidence interval.

estimation
> The process of inferring the parameters of a distribution from a sample.

estimator
> A statistic used to estimate a parameter.

maximum likelihood estimator
> An estimator that computes the point estimate with the highest likelihood.

mean squared error
> A measure of estimation error.

point estimate
> An estimate expressed as a single value.

CHAPTER 9

Correlation

Standard Scores

In this chapter, we look at relationships between variables. For example, we have a sense that height is related to weight; people who are taller tend to be heavier. *Correlation* is a description of this kind of relationship.

A challenge in measuring correlation is that the variables we want to compare might not be expressed in the same units. For example, height might be in centimeters and weight in kilograms. And even if they are in the same units, they come from different distributions.

There are two common solutions to these problems:

1. Transform all values to *standard scores*. This leads to the Pearson coefficient of correlation.
2. Transform all values to their percentile ranks. This leads to the Spearman coefficient.

If X is a series of values, x_i, we can convert to standard scores by subtracting the mean and dividing by the standard deviation: $z_i = (x_i - \mu) / \sigma$.

The numerator is a deviation: the distance from the mean. Dividing by σ *normalizes* the deviation, so the values of Z are dimensionless (no units) and their distribution has mean 0 and variance 1.

If X is normally distributed, so is Z; but if X is skewed or has outliers, so does Z. In those cases, it is more robust to use percentile ranks. If R contains the percentile ranks of the values in X, the distribution of R is uniform between 0 and 100, regardless of the distribution of X.

Covariance

Covariance is a measure of the tendency of two variables to vary together. If we have two series, X and Y, their deviations from the mean are

$$dx_i = x_i - \mu_X$$

$$dy_i = y_i - \mu_Y$$

where μ_X is the mean of X and μ_Y is the mean of Y. If X and Y vary together, their deviations tend to have the same sign.

If we multiply them together, the product is positive when the deviations have the same sign and negative when they have the opposite sign. So adding up the products gives a measure of the tendency to vary together.

Covariance is the mean of these products:

$$Cov(X,Y) = \frac{1}{n}\sum dx_i dy_i$$

where *n* is the length of the two series (they have to be the same length).

Covariance is useful in some computations, but it is seldom reported as a summary statistic because it is hard to interpret. Among other problems, its units are the product of the units of X and Y. So the covariance of weight and height might be in units of kilogram-meters, which doesn't mean much.

Exercise 9-1.

Write a function called Cov that takes two lists and computes their covariance. To test your function, compute the covariance of a list with itself and confirm that Cov(X, X) = Var(X).

You can download a solution from *http://thinkstats.com/correlation.py*.

Correlation

One solution to this problem is to divide the deviations by σ, which yields standard scores, and compute the product of standard scores:

$$p_i = \frac{(x_i - \mu_X)}{\sigma_X}\frac{(y_i - \mu_Y)}{\sigma_Y}$$

The mean of these products is

$$\rho = \frac{1}{n} \sum p_i$$

This value is called *Pearson's correlation* after Karl Pearson, an influential early statistician. It is easy to compute and easy to interpret. Because standard scores are dimensionless, so is ρ.

Also, the result is necessarily between –1 and +1. To see why, we can rewrite ρ by factoring out σ_X and σ_Y:

$$\rho = \frac{Cov(X, Y)}{\sigma_X \sigma_Y}$$

Expressed in terms of deviations, we have

$$\rho = \frac{\sum dx_i dy_x}{\sum dx_i \sum dy_i}$$

Then, by the ever-useful Cauchy-Schwarz inequality,[1] we can show that $\rho^2 \leq 1$, so $-1 \leq \rho \leq 1$.

The magnitude of ρ indicates the strength of the correlation. If $\rho = 1$, the variables are perfectly correlated, which means that if you know one, you can make a perfect prediction about the other. The same is also true if $\rho = -1$. It means that the variables are negatively correlated, but for purposes of prediction, a negative correlation is just as good as a positive one.

Most correlation in the real world is not perfect, but it is still useful. For example, if you know someone's height, you might be able to guess their weight. You might not get it exactly right, but your guess will be better than if you didn't know the height. Pearson's correlation is a measure of how much better.

So if $\rho = 0$, does that mean there is no relationship between the variables? Unfortunately, no. Pearson's correlation only measures *linear* relationships. If there's a nonlinear relationship, ρ understates the strength of the dependence.

Figure 9-1 is from *http://wikipedia.org/wiki/Correlation_and_dependence*. It shows scatterplots and correlation coefficients for several carefully-constructed datasets.

1. See *http://wikipedia.org/wiki/Cauchy-Schwarz_inequality*.

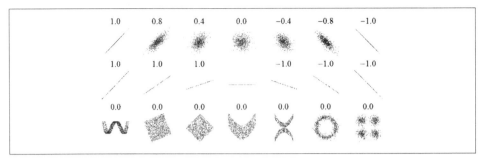

Figure 9-1. Examples of datasets with a range of correlations

The top row shows linear relationships with a range of correlations; you can use this row to get a sense of what different values of ρ look like. The second row shows perfect correlations with a range of slopes, which demonstrates that correlation is unrelated to slope (we'll talk about estimating slope soon). The third row shows variables that are clearly related, but because the relationship is non-linear, the correlation coefficient is 0.

The moral of this story is that you should always look at a scatterplot of your data before blindly computing a correlation coefficient.

Exercise 9-2.

Write a function called `Corr` that takes two lists and computes their correlation. Hint: use `thinkstats.Var` and the `Cov` function you wrote in the previous exercise.

To test your function, compute the covariance of a list with itself and confirm that Corr(*X*, *X*) is 1. You can download a solution from *http://thinkstats.com/correlation.py*.

Making Scatterplots in Pyplot

The simplest way to check for a relationship between two variables is a scatterplot, but making a good scatterplot is not always easy. As an example, I'll plot weight versus height for the respondents in the BRFSS (see "The Lognormal Distribution" on page 42). pyplot provides a function named `scatter` that makes scatterplots:

```
import matplotlib.pyplot as pyplot
pyplot.scatter(heights, weights)
```

Figure 9-2 shows the result. Not surprisingly, it looks like there is a positive correlation: taller people tend to be heavier. But this is not the best representation of the data, because the data is packed into columns. The problem is that the heights were rounded to the nearest inch, converted to centimeters, and then rounded again. Some information is lost in translation.

We can't get that information back, but we can minimize the effect on the scatterplot by *jittering* the data, which means adding random noise to reverse the effect of rounding

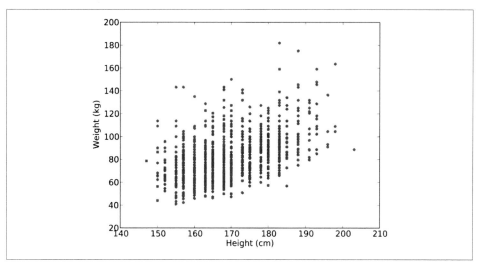

Figure 9-2. Simple scatterplot of weight versus height for the respondents in the BRFSS

off. Since these measurements were rounded to the nearest inch, they can be off by up to 0.5 inches or 1.3 cm. So I added uniform noise in the range –1.3 to 1.3:

```
jitter = 1.3
heights = [h + random.uniform(-jitter, jitter) for h in heights]
```

Figure 9-3 shows the result. Jittering the data makes the shape of the relationship clearer. In general, you should only jitter data for purposes of visualization and avoid using jittered data for analysis.

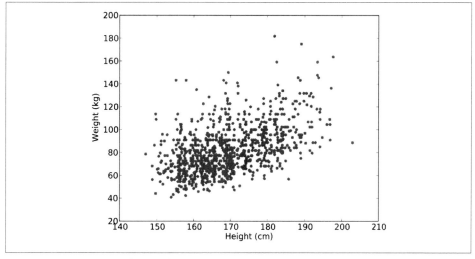

Figure 9-3. Scatterplot with jittered data

Even with jittering, this is not the best way to represent the data. There are many over-lapping points, which hides data in the dense parts of the figure and gives disproportionate emphasis to outliers.

We can solve that with the `alpha` parameter, which makes the points partly transparent:

```
pyplot.scatter(heights, weights, alpha=0.2)
```

Figure 9-4 shows the result. Overlapping data points look darker, so darkness is proportional to density. In this version of the plot, we can see an apparent artifact: a horizontal line near 90 kg or 200 pounds. Since this data is based on self-reports in pounds, the most likely explanation is some responses were rounded off (possibly down).

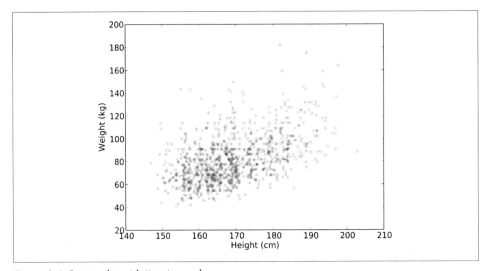

Figure 9-4. Scatterplot with jittering and transparency

Using transparency works well for moderate-sized datasets, but this figure only shows the first 1,000 records in the BRFSS, out of a total of 414,509.

To handle larger datasets, one option is a hexbin plot, which divides the graph into hexagonal bins and colors each bin according to how many data points fall in it. `pyplot` provides a function called `hexbin`:

```
pyplot.hexbin(heights, weights, cmap=matplotlib.cm.Blues)
```

Figure 9-5 shows the result with a blue colormap. An advantage of a hexbin is that it shows the shape of the relationship well, and it is efficient for large datasets. A drawback is that it makes the outliers invisible.

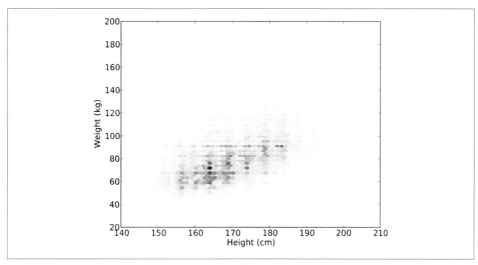

Figure 9-5. Scatterplot with binned data using pyplot.hexbin

The moral of this story is that it is not easy to make a scatterplot that is not potentially misleading. You can download the code for these figures from *http://thinkstats.com/brfss_scatter.py*.

Spearman's Rank Correlation

Pearson's correlation works well if the relationship between variables is linear and if the variables are roughly normal. But it is not robust in the presence of outliers.

Anscombe's quartet demonstrates this effect; it contains four datasets with the same correlation. One is a linear relation with random noise, one is a non-linear relation, one is a perfect relation with an outlier, and one has no relation except an artifact caused by an outlier. You can read more about it at *http://wikipedia.org/wiki/Anscombe's_quartet*.

Spearman's rank correlation is an alternative that mitigates the effect of outliers and skewed distributions. To compute Spearman's correlation, we have to compute the *rank* of each value, which is its index in the sorted sample. For example, in the sample {7, 1, 2, 5} the rank of the value 5 is 3, because it appears third if we sort the elements. Then we compute Pearson's correlation for the ranks.

An alternative to Spearman's is to apply a transform that makes the data more nearly normal, then compute Pearson's correlation for the transformed data. For example, if the data is approximately lognormal, you could take the log of each value and compute the correlation of the logs.

Exercise 9-3.

Write a function that takes a sequence and returns a list that contains the rank for each element. For example, if the sequence is {7, 1, 2, 5}, the result should be { 4, 1, 2, 3}.

If the same value appears more than once, the strictly correct solution is to assign each of them the average of their ranks. But if you ignore that and assign them ranks in arbitrary order, the error is usually small.

Write a function that takes two sequences (with the same length) and computes their Spearman rank coefficient. You can download a solution from *http://thinkstats.com/ correlation.py*.

Exercise 9-4.

Download *http://thinkstats.com/brfss.py* and *http://thinkstats.com/brfss_scatter.py*. Run them and confirm that you can read the BRFSS data and generate scatterplots.

Comparing the scatterplots to Figure 9-1, what value do you expect for Pearson's correlation? What value do you get?

Because the distribution of adult weight is lognormal, there are outliers that affect the correlation. Try plotting log(weight) versus height, and compute Pearson's correlation for the transformed variable.

Finally, compute Spearman's rank correlation for weight and height. Which coefficient do you think is the best measure of the strength of the relationship? You can download a solution from *http://thinkstats.com/brfss_corr.py*.

Least Squares Fit

Correlation coefficients measure the strength and sign of a relationship, but not the slope. There are several ways to estimate the slope; the most common is a *linear least squares fit*. A "linear fit" is a line intended to model the relationship between variables. A "least squares" fit is one that minimizes the mean squared error (MSE) between the line and the data.[2]

Suppose we have a sequence of points, Y, that we want to express as a function of another sequence X. If there is a linear relationship between X and Y with intercept α and slope β, we expect each y_i to be roughly $\alpha + \beta x_i$.

But unless the correlation is perfect, this prediction is only approximate. The deviation, or *residual*, is

$$\varepsilon_i = (\alpha + \beta x_i) - y_i$$

2. See *http://wikipedia.org/wiki/Simple_linear_regression*.

The residual might be due to random factors like measurement error, or non-random factors that are unknown. For example, if we are trying to predict weight as a function of height, unknown factors might include diet, exercise, and body type.

If we get the parameters α and β wrong, the residuals get bigger, so it makes intuitive sense that the parameters we want are the ones that minimize the residuals.

As usual, we could minimize the absolute value of the residuals, or their squares, or their cubes, etc. The most common choice is to minimize the sum of squared residuals.

$$\min_{\alpha,\beta} \sum \varepsilon_i^2$$

Why? There are three good reasons and one bad one:

- Squaring has the obvious feature of treating positive and negative residuals the same, which is usually what we want.
- Squaring gives more weight to large residuals, but not so much weight that the largest residual always dominates.
- If the residuals are independent of x, random, and normally distributed with $\mu = 0$ and constant (but unknown) σ, then the least squares fit is also the maximum likelihood estimator of α and β.[3]
- The values of $\hat{\alpha}$ and $\hat{\beta}$ that minimize the squared residuals can be computed efficiently.

That last reason made sense when computational efficiency was more important than choosing the method most appropriate to the problem at hand. That's no longer the case, so it is worth considering whether squared residuals are the right thing to minimize.

For example, if you are using values of X to predict values of Y, guessing too high might be better (or worse) than guessing too low. In that case, you might want to compute some cost function, cost(ε_i), and minimize total cost.

However, computing a least squares fit is quick, easy, and often good enough, so here's how:

1. Compute the sample means, $\bar{x}$ and $\bar{y}$, the variance of X, and the covariance of X and Y.

2. The estimated slope is

$$\hat{\beta} = \frac{Cov(X, Y)}{Var(X)}$$

3. And the intercept is

---

3. See Press et al., *Numerical Recipes in C*, Chapter 15 at *http://www.nrbook.com/a/bookcpdf/c15-1.pdf*.

$$\hat{\alpha} = \bar{y} - \hat{\beta}\bar{x}$$

To see how this is derived, you can read *http://wikipedia.org/wiki/Numerical_methods _for_linear_least_squares*.

Exercise 9-5.

Write a function named `LeastSquares` that takes X and Y and computes $\hat{\alpha}$ and $\hat{\beta}$. You can download a solution from *http://thinkstats.com/correlation.py*.

Exercise 9-6.

Using the data from the BRFSS again, compute the linear least squares fit for log(weight) versus height. You can download a solution from *http://thinkstats.com/brfss_corr.py*.

Exercise 9-7.

The distribution of wind speeds in a given location determines the wind power density, which is an upper bound on the average power that a wind turbine at that location can generate. According to some sources, empirical distributions of wind speed are well modeled by a Weibull distribution (see *http://wikipedia.org/wiki/Wind_power#Distri bution_of_wind_speed*).

To evaluate whether a location is a viable site for a wind turbine, you can set up an anemometer to measure wind speed for a period of time. But it is hard to measure the tail of the wind speed distribution accurately because, by definition, events in the tail don't happen very often.

One way to address this problem is to use measurements to estimate the parameters of a Weibull distribution, then integrate over the continuous PDF to compute wind power density.

To estimate the parameters of a Weibull distribution, we can use the transformation from Exercise 4-6 and then use a linear fit to find the slope and intercept of the trans-formed data.

Write a function that takes a sample from a Weibull distribution and estimates its parameters.

Now write a function that takes the parameters of a Weibull distribution of wind speed and computes average wind power density (you might have to do some research for this part).

Goodness of Fit

Having fit a linear model to the data, we might want to know how good it is. Well, that depends on what it's for. One way to evaluate a model is its predictive power.

In the context of prediction, the quantity we are trying to guess is called a *dependent variable* and the quantity we are using to make the guess is called an *explanatory* or *independent variable*.

To measure the predictive power of a model, we can compute the *coefficient of determination*, more commonly known as "R-squared":

$$R^2 = 1 - \frac{Var(\varepsilon)}{Var(Y)}$$

To understand what R^2 means, suppose (again) that you are trying to guess someone's weight. If you didn't know anything about them, your best strategy would be to guess $\bar{y}$; in that case the MSE of your guesses would be $Var(Y)$:

$$MSE = \frac{1}{n} \sum (\bar{y} - y_i)^2 = Var(Y)$$

But if I told you their height, you would guess $\hat{\alpha} + \hat{\beta} x_i$; in that case your MSE would be $Var(\varepsilon)$.

$$MSE = \frac{1}{n} \sum (\hat{\alpha} + \hat{\beta} x_i - y_i)^2 = Var(\varepsilon)$$

So the term $Var(\varepsilon)/Var(Y)$ is the ratio of mean squared error with and without the explanatory variable, which is the fraction of variability left unexplained by the model. The complement, R^2, is the fraction of variability explained by the model.

If a model yields $R^2 = 0.64$, you could say that the model explains 64% of the variability, or it might be more precise to say that it reduces the MSE of your predictions by 64%.

In the context of a linear least squares model, it turns out that there is a simple relationship between the coefficient of determination and Pearson's correlation coefficient, ρ:

$$R^2 = \rho^2$$

See *http://wikipedia.org/wiki/Howzzat!*

Exercise 9-8.

The Wechsler Adult Intelligence Scale (WAIS) is meant to be a measure of intelligence; scores are calibrated so that the mean and standard deviation in the general population are 100 and 15.

Suppose that you wanted to predict someone's WAIS score based on their SAT scores. According to one study, there is a Pearson correlation of 0.72 between total SAT scores and WAIS scores.

If you applied your predictor to a large sample, what would you expect to be the mean squared error (MSE) of your predictions?

Hint: What is the MSE if you always guess 100?

Exercise 9-9.

Write a function named `Residuals` that takes X, Y, $\hat{\alpha}$ and $\hat{\beta}$ and returns a list of ε_i.

Write a function named `CoefDetermination` that takes the ε_i and Y and returns R^2. To test your functions, confirm that $R^2 = \rho^2$. You can download a solution from *http://thinkstats.com/correlation.py*.

Exercise 9-10.

Using the height and weight data from the BRFSS (one more time), compute $\hat{\alpha}$, $\hat{\beta}$ and R^2. If you were trying to guess someone's weight, how much would it help to know their height? You can download a solution from *http://thinkstats.com/brfss_corr.py*.

Correlation and Causation

In general, a relationship between two variables does not tell you whether one causes the other, or the other way around, or both, or whether they might both be caused by something else altogether (see xkcd web comic (*http://xkcd.com/552/*)).

This rule can be summarized with the phrase "Correlation does not imply causation," which is so pithy it has its own Wikipedia page: *http://wikipedia.org/wiki/Correlation _does_not_imply_causation*.

So what can you do to provide evidence of causation?

1. Use time. If A comes before B, then A can cause B but not the other way around (at least according to our common understanding of causation). The order of events can help us infer the direction of causation, but it does not preclude the possibility that something else causes both A and B.

2. Use randomness. If you divide a large population into two groups at random and compute the means of almost any variable, you expect the difference to be small. This is a consequence of the Central Limit Theorem (so it is subject to the same requirements).

If the groups are nearly identical in all variable but one, you can eliminate spurious relationships.

This works even if you don't know what the relevant variables are, but it works even better if you do, because you can check that the groups are identical.

These ideas are the motivation for the *randomized controlled trial*, in which subjects are assigned randomly to two (or more) groups: a *treatment* group that receives some kind of intervention, like a new medicine, and a *control group* that receives no intervention, or another treatment whose effects are known.

A randomized controlled trial is the most reliable way to demonstrate a causal relationship, and the foundation of science-based medicine (see *http://wikipedia.org/wiki/Randomized_controlled_trial*).

Unfortunately, controlled trials are only possible in the laboratory sciences, medicine, and a few other disciplines. In the social sciences, controlled experiments are rare, usually because they are impossible or unethical.

One alternative is to look for a *natural experiment*, where different "treatments" are applied to groups that are otherwise similar. One danger of natural experiments is that the groups might differ in ways that are not apparent. You can read more about this topic at *http://wikipedia.org/wiki/Natural_experiment*.

In some cases it is possible to infer causal relationships using *regression analysis*. A linear least squares fit is a simple form of regression that explains a dependent variable using one explanatory variable. There are similar techniques that work with arbitrary numbers of independent variables.

I won't cover those techniques here, but there are also simple ways to control for spurious relationships. For example, in the NSFG, we saw that first babies tend to be lighter than others (see "Back to the Survey Data" on page 29). But birth weight is also correlated with the mother's age, and mothers of first babies tend to be younger than mothers of other babies.

So it may be that first babies are lighter because their mothers are younger. To control for the effect of age, we could divide the mothers into age groups and compare birth weights for first babies and others in each age group.

If the difference between first babies and others is the same in each age group as it was in the pooled data, we conclude that the difference is not related to age. If there is no difference, we conclude that the effect is entirely due to age. Or, if the difference is smaller, we can quantify how much of the effect is due to age.

Exercise 9-11.

The NSFG data includes a variable named `agepreg` that records the age of the mother at the time of birth. Make a scatterplot of mother's age and baby's weight for each live birth. Can you see a relationship?

Compute a linear least-squares fit for these variables. What are the units of the estimated parameters $\hat{\alpha}$ and $\hat{\beta}$? How would you summarize these results in a sentence or two?

Compute the average age for mothers of first babies and the average age of other mothers. Based on the difference in ages between the groups, how much difference do you expect in the mean birth weights? What fraction of the actual difference in birth weights is explained by the difference in ages?

You can download a solution to this problem from *http://thinkstats.com/agemodel.py*. If you are curious about multivariate regression, you can run *http://thinkstats.com/age_lm.py* which shows how to use the R statistical computing package from Python. But that's a whole other book.

Glossary

coefficient of determination
> A measure of the goodness of fit of a linear model.

control group
> A group in a controlled trial that receives no treatment, or a treatment whose effect is known.

correlation
> a description of the dependence between variables.

covariance
> a measure of the tendency of two variables to vary together.

dependent variable
> A variable we are trying to predict or explain.

independent variable
> A variable we are using to predict a dependent variable, also called an explanatory variable.

least squares fit
> A model of a dataset that minimizes the sum of squares of the residuals.

natural experiment
> An experimental design that takes advantage of a natural division of subjects into groups in ways that are at least approximately random.

normalize
> To transform a set of values so that their mean is 0 and their variance is 1.

randomized controlled trial
> An experimental design in which subject are divided into groups at random, and different groups are given different treatments.

rank
> The index where an element appears in a sorted list.

residual
> A measure of the deviation of an actual value from a model.

standard score
> A value that has been normalized.

treatment
> An change or intervention applied to one group in a controlled trial.

Index

A
abstraction, 44
Adams, Cecil, 21
Adult Intelligence Scale, 40, 108
adult weight, 42, 43, 104
agemodel.py, 110
age_lm.py, 110
analysis, 44, 67, 80, 81
anecdotal evidence, 2, 8
Anscombe's quartet, 103
apparent effect, 7, 8, 19, 73
artifact, 7, 8
Australia, 33
average, 11, 62

B
bar plot, 14, 17
baseball, 54
basketball, 54
Bayes factor, 79
Bayesian estimation, 70, 89, 94
Bayesian probability, 77, 79
Bayesianism, 47, 58, 89
Bayes's theorem, 56
Behavioral Risk Factor Surveillance System, 42, 43, 52, 100, 104, 106, 108
belief, 48, 58, 79
bias
    confirmation, 2
    oversampling, 24
    selection, 2, 24
biased estimator, 87, 88, 95
bin, 19, 21, 70
binning, 25

binomial coefficient, 53
binomial distribution, 53
birth time, 33
birth weight, 25, 29, 30, 31, 32, 39, 41, 62, 78, 109
birthday, 36
bisection algorithm, 28
Blue Man Group, 65
booyah, 66
bread police, 51
BRFSS, 42, 43, 52, 100, 104, 106, 108
brfss.py, 43, 104
brfss_corr.py, 104, 106, 108
brfss_figs.py, 43
brfss_scatter.py, 103, 104
Brisbane, 33

C
cancer cluster, 55
casino, 81
Cauchy-Schwarz inequality, 99
causation, 108
CCDF, 34, 35, 37, 44
CDF, 26, 27, 32, 36, 38, 42, 45, 62, 64, 70
    complementary, 34, 35, 37, 44
Cdf object, 28
Cdf.py, 28, 29, 31
cell, 80, 83
censored data, 92, 95
Central Limit Theorem, 68, 70
central tendency, 11, 21, 32
ch-square test, 83
chance, 73, 76
chapeau, 5
chi-square distribution, 89

We'd like to hear your suggestions for improving our indexes. Send email to *index@oreilly.com*.

jitter, 100
Journal of the American Medical Association, 56

L

Lake Wobegon effect, 62
Langan, Christopher, 40
least squares fit, 104, 110
length, pregnancy, 7, 15, 17, 18, 20, 40, 62, 73, 74, 75, 78, 80, 81
likelihood, 56, 58, 79, 91
likelihood ratio, 79, 83
line plot, 17
linear least squares, 104
linear regression, 104
linear relationship, 99
linear transformation, 67
locomotive problem, 93
locomotive.py, 94, 95
logarithm, 69
logarithmic scale, 35, 37
lognormal distribution, 42, 43, 52, 68, 69, 103, 104
longitudinal study, 3, 9

M

MacKay, David, 58, 79, 92
map, 13
margin of error, 92
margin of victory, 92
Martin, Steve, 5
mass, 64
matplotlib, 14
max, 67
maximum likelihood estimator, 86, 88, 93, 96, 105
mean, 11, 17, 33, 68, 80, 85, 86, 88, 97
    trimmed, 19
    truncated, 19
mean squared error, 86, 93, 96
mean, difference in, 74, 81
median, 32, 33, 37, 85, 86, 88
medicine, 109
method, init, 5, 63
Minnesota Senate Race, 92
MLE, 86, 88, 93, 96, 105
Mlodinow, Leonard, 49
mode, 14, 15, 22

model, 40, 41, 43, 44, 46
moment of inertia, 64
Monte Carlo, 54, 59, 80
Monty Hall
    confused, 51
    problem, 50
Mosteller, Frederick, 93
MSE, 86, 93, 96
Munroe, Randall, 108
mutually exclusive, 52
myplot.py, 15, 29

N

National Survey of Family Growth, 3, 4, 18, 19, 25, 29, 31, 39, 73, 74, 75, 76, 77, 78, 81, 109
natural experiment, 109, 110
noise, 101
normal distribution, 38, 40, 41, 43, 51, 64, 65, 67, 68, 69, 70, 81, 85, 86, 87, 97, 103
normal probability plot, 40, 46
normalization, 13, 22
normalize, 97, 110
normalizing constant, 56, 59
NSFG, 3, 4, 18, 19, 25, 29, 31, 39, 73, 74, 75, 76, 77, 78, 81, 109
null hypothesis, 73, 74, 79, 83

O

oeuf, 5
one-sided test, 77, 83
operations on distributions, 61
outlier, 15, 18, 22, 61, 85, 88, 102, 104
oversampling, 4, 9, 24

P

p-value, 73, 74, 82, 83
parameter, 33, 36, 37, 38, 42, 44, 45, 85, 88, 89
Pareto distribution, 36, 37, 40, 43, 44, 68, 69
Pareto World, 37
Pareto, Vilfredo, 36
particles, 92
PDF, 64, 65, 70, 91, 106
Pearson coefficient of correlation, 97, 99, 103
Pearson, Karl, 99
Pearson's median skewness coefficient, 61

Z

Zipf's law, 37

About the Author

Allen Downey is an Associate Professor of Computer Science at the Olin College of Engineering. He has taught computer science at Wellesley College, Colby College, and U.C. Berkeley. He has a Ph.D. in Computer Science from U.C. Berkeley and Master's and Bachelor's degrees from MIT.

Colophon

The animal on the cover of *Think Stats*, first edition, is an archerfish.

The cover image is from *Dover*. The cover font is Adobe ITC Garamond. The text font is Linotype Birka; the heading font is Adobe Myriad Condensed; and the code font is LucasFont's TheSansMonoCondensed.

Get even more for your money.

Join the O'Reilly Community, and register the O'Reilly books you own. It's free, and you'll get:

- $4.99 ebook upgrade offer
- 40% upgrade offer on O'Reilly print books
- Membership discounts on books and events
- Free lifetime updates to ebooks and videos
- Multiple ebook formats, DRM FREE
- Participation in the O'Reilly community
- Newsletters
- Account management
- 100% Satisfaction Guarantee

Signing up is easy:

1. **Go to: oreilly.com/go/register**
2. **Create an O'Reilly login.**
3. **Provide your address.**
4. **Register your books.**

Note: English-language books only

To order books online:
oreilly.com/store

For questions about products or an order:
orders@oreilly.com

To sign up to get topic-specific email announcements and/or news about upcoming books, conferences, special offers, and new technologies:
elists@oreilly.com

For technical questions about book content:
booktech@oreilly.com

To submit new book proposals to our editors:
proposals@oreilly.com

O'Reilly books are available in multiple DRM-free ebook formats. For more information:
oreilly.com/ebooks

O'REILLY®

Spreading the knowledge of innovators | oreilly.com

The information you need, when and where you need it.

With Safari Books Online, you can:

Access the contents of thousands of technology and business books

- Quickly search over 7000 books and certification guides
- Download whole books or chapters in PDF format, at no extra cost, to print or read on the go
- Copy and paste code
- Save up to 35% on O'Reilly print books
- **New!** Access mobile-friendly books directly from cell phones and mobile devices

Stay up-to-date on emerging topics before the books are published

- Get on-demand access to evolving manuscripts.
- Interact directly with authors of upcoming books

Explore thousands of hours of video on technology and design topics

- Learn from expert video tutorials
- Watch and replay recorded conference sessions

Spreading the knowledge of innovators   safari.oreilly.com

Lightning Source UK Ltd.
Milton Keynes UK
UKOW02f1308250713

214312UK00003B/165/P